TWO FAMILIES AND FOUR GENERATIONS

JAMES BUTLER, JR.

TWO FAMILIES

AND FOUR

GENERATIONS

A STORY OF WEALTH, FAITH,
AND RESILIENCE

LIONCREST
PUBLISHING

TWO FAMILIES AND FOUR GENERATIONS
A Story of Wealth, Faith, and Resilience

FIRST EDITION

ISBN 978-1-5445-4245-4 *Hardcover*
      978-1-5445-4243-0 *Paperback*
      978-1-5445-4244-7 *Ebook*

FOR MY MOTHER AND FATHER

FOR EVANGELINE CANNING FOGARTY

FOR MARGARET HERBRUCK BUTLER

CONTENTS

INTRODUCTION

THIS IS A STORY OF FAITH, MONEY, AND PRIVILEGE IN one American family. It's about what gets passed down from generation to generation, and the values that shape us.

It's also a tale of the expectations and responsibilities that come with wealth. By the time of my own birth in 1942, money and success had already become the standard on both sides of my family.

My great-grandfather James Butler was the classic American success story, an Irish immigrant without any connections or money, building a fortune from nothing. Known as the original "Butter and Eggs" man, he built a large chain of grocery stores and went on to invest in other ventures, including thoroughbred racetracks.

On my mother's side, my grandfather William Ewing was one of the founding partners at Morgan Stanley. On both sides of the family, the early part of the twentieth century was a time of growing fortune, and the privilege that came along with it.

Both these men, my paternal great-grandfather, and my maternal grandfather, worked hard for business success, and attained it on a wide scale. They both used a portion of their money for the faith causes they cared about, but also passed on significant wealth to their descendants. What became of each of those fortunes is part of this story too. Money brings with it great privilege and opens many doors; it also can have a dark side that can cause conflict in families and create burdens of expectation.

And of course, wealth doesn't protect you from great suffering or insulate you from tragedy.

My paternal grandfather (the firstborn son of the original Butter and Eggs man), would die at the age of fifty in a horse-riding accident. And his son (my father) would also pass away at age fifty-one, weeks after hearing that his first grandchild had been born, but never having had a chance to meet him. Both of these men would also struggle mightily with alcohol.

I escaped the curse of alcoholism, but it seemed I might not escape the fate of a death in my early fifties. I was involved in a boating accident at age fifty-two that came very close to making me the third generation of James Butlers to die too young. And being Irish, I couldn't help but have the thought of a family curse. If it was a curse, I somehow escaped that too.

I awoke from the nightmare of that accident and learned I had suffered a traumatic brain injury, one that permanently altered my world. But nonetheless, I lived to tell the tale, and with love and support from family, I recovered sufficiently to appreciate the joys and sufferings of life once again. It was a different life but very much worth living.

Part of what helped me through the years after my accident was the family's spiritual tradition, which is Roman Catholic. This spiritual thread runs through the generations imperfectly, but it's there. My great-grandfather James Butler's first cousin Johanna Butler became a famous nun here in America, and both sides of the family provided significant financial support to the Church and its missions.

While acknowledging and mourning the Church's shortcomings, it has still served as a bulwark and a touchstone throughout the generations of my family, and in my own life, and it will be a part of this story too.

WHY I'M TELLING THIS STORY

I'm in my eighties now. Going all the way back to high school, I've had a love of history, and even briefly flirted with the idea of training to become a history professor.

In many ways, this book is my attempt to reckon with my own history, to see who came behind me, and to hold my own life up and measure it. It's something I hope the generations after me will read to get a sense of the past.

I also can't help but think of the families I've known over the years, many privileged similarly to mine, who have also known many triumphs and trials through their own generations. In reading about my family's experiences, perhaps they'll recognize their own, and it will aid them as they live and think about their own lives.

I'm also writing to the generation following mine, the ones who are middle aged and beginning to grapple with the accomplishments of their life, but also the regrets. Telling each other our histories can help us put those accomplishments in perspective and perhaps help us go easier on ourselves about our regrets.

And finally, I write this for my grandchildren's generation, and those who come after. Many things have changed, and the old customs, hierarchies, and social clubs have mostly passed away. That might be mostly for the good, but things get lost too, and maybe this book can help newer generations to understand what it was like to grow up at a different time.

My hope for this book is that it can pass on wisdom to others. Through its many stories, I hope the positive values of duty, faith, and helping others shine through. Most of all, the great value of resilience in the face of suffering and setbacks.

As you'll read in the first chapter, my wife and I would need as much resilience as possible when our lives changed forever in September 1994.

CHAPTER 1

THE ACCIDENT

ON OCTOBER 3, 1994, I AWOKE IN A HOSPITAL ROOM. I was fifty-two years old, but an accident three days before had given me a traumatic brain injury that temporarily had given me the mental acuity of an eight-year-old. I also would spend some of my hospital stay wandering the hall thinking I was a Catholic priest.

The chain of events that put me in that state began on an ordinary Friday afternoon. My wife Margot and I got together with a friend of my mother's for an evening on the water. Billy Cox owned a Mako 21 powerboat with a big outboard motor. We made plans to cross Long Island Sound and return that evening. The trip wouldn't take long in a powerboat.

But our plans changed later in the day after Margot stopped by the Belle Haven Club in Greenwich. She mentioned our plans to go out on the water to the club's harbor master. Because the water was quite choppy that day, the official advised Margot against it. "It's a good idea if you don't go out today—particularly if you're going out in the late afternoon."

So instead, we decided to drive the twelve miles to Rowayton, Connecticut and meet Billy and his girlfriend, Beth, for dinner. We enjoyed dinner with them and after the meal, although it was about 10 p.m., the four of us decided that Billy would take us out for a ride in his boat after all. The waters in the Sound had calmed down considerably and it sounded like a relaxing way to finish off a pleasant evening.

We hopped in Billy's boat and rode down the coastline. Although by now it was nearly 11 p.m., we stopped at a hotel on the waterfront in Greenwich to see if any of our friends were there before we headed back to Rowayton. Looking back now, it seems kind of silly that we were traveling this much, but hindsight is always 20/20.

The inn was busy. While we did see some familiar faces, it was too crowded and too loud. In those days, the hotel had also become a meeting place for anyone who wanted to find a "professional." There were several of these women circulating about. We added up this whole scene and decided we wouldn't stay. Billy didn't have anything to drink at the hotel, I may have had a beer, and Margot and Beth had dessert. It was time to go.

Once we got back to the boat, we headed up the coast. We were near Stamford, not far from Long Neck Point, when the accident happened. Floating in that part of the Sound was a commercial mooring buoy that had been there for years. (These types of buoys are used for temporary off-shore and remote moorings for barges and other vessels.)

There had been ongoing issues with the buoy's night lighting. This problem had been reported in the past by other boaters and sailors, but we didn't find that out until after the accident.

The four of us were all eager to get back to Rowayton—Margot and I still had to drive home from there. So, we were motoring at a good clip. There were few lights to be seen along the coastline and the moon was waning. Both the sea and the night sky were quite dark as we headed north. Because of the dark, it was hard to see anything in the water—and without a working light the buoy was invisible. None of us saw the buoy coming when we struck it traveling at twenty knots an hour.

At impact, Margot and Billy were both thrown out of the boat in a forward direction. Billy missed the buoy and landed in the water, fortunately avoiding serious injury. Margot wasn't as lucky. She struck something in the boat as she was thrown forward.

Although she was knocked unconscious, some part of her mind remained alert enough to realize that something perilous was happening. She has told me that in her mind's eye, she saw herself in a dark tunnel. At the end of the tunnel there was a light—and she was moving toward it.

She was pulled back to consciousness when Billy reached out and grabbed her. They had been thrown in the water not far from each other. Billy was able to swim to her and he pulled her over to the buoy. Although the object was covered in seaweed and barnacles, he instructed her to hold on to it while he swam back to retrieve the boat with me and Beth still aboard that was drifting away. Thankfully, the engine had shifted into neutral when the key, which was kept on a lanyard, had been pulled out of the engine during the collision.

Billy was able to reach the boat. It was leaking a bit, but he got it started and returned to pick up Margot. Because both Beth and I were unconscious, he instructed Margot to sit in the back and hold our heads out of the water.

Billy got us back up to Five Mile River—or at least close enough. As he steered the boat to shore, he called for help on the radio. When we pulled into a boatyard, we were met by two ambulances that took us straight to the Norwalk Hospital emergency room.

Margot was treated for her injuries, Beth had several broken bones set, and I was in a subconscious state. The doctor on duty that night later remarked that after seeing the three of us in the emergency room, he did not know how all of us came out alive.

The hospital had set up a triage unit when we arrived at the emergency room. I was by far the worst. Although Margot had a head wound and other injuries, she still knew exactly what happened. I had no memory of the event.

Beth was discharged after a week or so. Margot had been

there for just a day or two, but she suffered from insipid diabetes as a result of the accident. I was in that hospital for a month.

It turned out that I had a concussion on the left side of my head. There was a scar and somehow it caused water on my brain. Doctors thought I needed an incision to drain the water. The attending surgeon in the emergency room had to decide: Should he operate and relieve the pressure? Or give it a few days to let the water dissipate on its own?

The operation had its own risks, so the consensus was to wait. I remained unconscious for three days. But just as the doctors were again considering the surgery, I woke up on the third night.

As I regained consciousness that night, I became aware that I was in a little room with another patient next to me separated by a curtain. Although I still knew who I was, I was otherwise quite out of it. It felt as if I had gone back many years into the past and something bad had happened to me. I thought I was in bed because I was sick, just like when I was a little kid. When people came to visit me, I felt as if I was a school child.

Everyone was extremely kind. They tried to reassure me, saying things softly like, "Oh, you've had this accident." And as soon as my mother and Margot (who needed some recovery time of her own) were able to visit, they came regularly to see me. Other family members and relatives also visited. One uncle, my mother's brother, Uncle Bill, made sure that the hospital had a good doctor looking after me.

It is times like this where you realize that family is the foundation for resilience. Of course, our relationships were as complicated and imperfect as in most families. But when I desperately needed help, here were both my mom and Uncle Bill providing emotional and financial support.

No one was more key in helping me during my long recovery than my wife Margot. It could not have been easy for her, injured herself and taking on the burden of the uncertainty of my condition and our future.

After I was able to get up and move around a bit, I would wear a green cotton robe that Margot brought for me. In my walks around the hospital, I'd see many other people and smile at them. In my mind, I knew they were there to help me. So, whenever I saw them, I'd smile and say, "God bless you," or something similar. One or two of them asked Margot if I thought I was a priest.

My wife says it did seem as if in my own mind I may have thought myself to be a cleric. According to her, it was almost as if I had moved into another world. I didn't seem to realize what had happened to me or what a horrific accident I had survived. Perhaps I had temporarily entered a spiritual mindset to protect myself from the harshness of my condition. At that point, I didn't have much recollection of my life before the accident, and I soon concluded that my entire future was reliant upon my faith in God.

That future and the extent of my recovery was still uncertain back then. I will share more about what happened next in the book's final chapter, but first I want to travel back several generations.

Both my paternal great-grandfather and my maternal grandfather made significant marks in the world of business, and passed down money and lessons through the generations. The example of their lives and the fortunes they built would have a big impact on their descendants, including of course, my one life.

CHAPTER 2

THE SQUIRE

IN 1875, IRELAND WAS A POOR AND STRUGGLING COUN-
try, but in the United States, the Industrial Age had begun,
and the nation was undergoing explosive growth. Newly
developed machinery and factory production lines were
desperate for workers. It was that year my great-grandfather, James Butler, joined the throngs of Irish immigrants
who arrived in Boston, Massachusetts seeking a new life.

Born in 1855, James grew up in Kilkenny County on
property the Butler family had been farming for fifteen
generations. They were fairly successful farmers, and the
children were educated in a parish school in the nearby
town of Russelltown. When James was twenty, he inherited
about one hundred pounds from an uncle. That same year,
with his inheritance in his pocket, he said goodbye to his
parents and sailed for America.

When he arrived in Boston, James initially worked on a
farm near Goshen Mountain, Massachusetts, but soon

after left the rural life to join an older brother in Illinois who had emigrated before him. James went to work with his brother at a hotel in Urbana, Illinois That too, lasted for only a short period because soon after, he landed a job at the distinguished Sherman House Hotel in Chicago. Here was where this ambitious young man was introduced to the food service and entertainment industries. He learned how to purchase, prepare, and safely store food.

According to a June 2020 article, "The Egg and Butter Man of East View," in the *River City Journal* written by Tarrytown, New York historian, Richard Miller, the confidence, skills, and experience the industrious young immigrant gained in Chicago prepared him well to find work in New York City as the head steward at Manhattan's Windsor Hotel. He so excelled in the position that in 1885 when President Grover Cleveland was inaugurated, James was sent to Washington, DC to supervise the inaugural dinner. The memory of the hectic evening remained with him for the rest of his life. "I was the busiest man in the United States that night," he would say. Years later, in 1909, he would be invited to attend President Taft's inaugural events as a guest. He declined, telling his family, "I don't even like to think about an inauguration."

From the Windsor Hotel, James moved on to work at the Murray Hill Hotel on Park Avenue. It was a successful job, and certainly one that would have seen him well established for the rest of his life. But fate intervened. Upon his arrival in New York, he rented a room at Mrs. O'Connor's boarding house. The landlady had a son named Patrick J. O'Connor. Patrick was a melancholy sort who ran a small grocery store in a rougher part of the city. In the evenings, sitting around the boarding house dinner table, Patrick would moan and complain about how bad business was and why he couldn't afford to move to a better location.

Finally, one evening, James Butler had heard enough. He turned to Patrick and said, "O'Connor, stop your complaining. How much do you need to work in a good part of town?" Patrick replied that it would take at least $2,000 to open a store in a more flourishing area.

James, who had by now become adept at practicing the art of a deal, told the young man, "All right, I will stake you." Together the two new partners searched for a better location. Eventually they found the ideal spot—a vacant building at 857 Second Avenue.

Since both men were Irish, they decided to paint the storefront a bright green. On September 2, 1882, P.J. O'Connor and Company opened its doors. While Patrick O'Connor worked as the face of the business, running the shop and day-to-day operations, James was responsible for the finances and purchasing the groceries. He was still working at the Windsor Hotel when the store opened, so after he made food purchases for the hotel, he would make a second purchase for the store. For a time, the young immigrant was very busy working for both the hotel and the grocery. But the little store with its kelly-green front and glittering gold lettering quickly began to prosper.

By 1883, the partners were able to purchase a second store at 10th and 44th Streets. Within just a few years, James

Butler was able to buy out O'Connor. He renamed the stores James Butler, Inc. He was twenty-nine and had figured out what he wanted to do with the rest of his life. He decided to open an entire chain of food stores. According to historian Miller, he purchased one store front after another—all of them in very select locations. The easily recognized storefronts were all painted with the same gold lettering over a green background. In a hand-up to other struggling immigrants—and a move to keep overhead costs down—every grocery was staffed with two young men, often hired right off the boat from Ireland.

By catering to—and gearing his prices to—what he referred to as the "carriage trade," he offered a greater-than-normal variety of food and sold only the very best quality groceries. He initially offered credit to his patrons and would deliver groceries to their homes. Eventually, however, as the number of stores he operated continued to grow, James decided that both credit and delivery services were "a lot of damn nonsense." He ended both practices, but still provided deliveries to a handful of older, housebound patrons.

His business practices were so successful that by 1909, he had more than 200 stores doing a brisk business of $15 million a year. By then, the Squire, as he had become known, had become the largest grocery chain operator in the United States. Eventually, he would open 1,100 stores and earn another title. The Squire would also be referred to as "The Original Butter and Eggs Man" in honor of his success in the grocery business.

As he was opening those stores, the young entrepreneur

was also accumulating an appreciable amount of real estate in New York City. By 1929, he had garnered a personal wealth of more than $30 million. He was also able to avoid losing that fortune by outwitting the stock market and selling $1 million worth of property at peak pre-crash prices.

According to Stephen Birmingham's book, *Real Lace: America's Irish Rich*, during James's time in New York City, the Squire did more than just spend his days amassing a fortune. In 1883, he married the lovely Mary A. Rorke. The young Irish woman would bear him eleven children before her untimely death in her early forties. Sadly, only four of the eleven children would survive to adulthood.

James was heartbroken at her death. He had long said that he had a four-part plan for his life: "To become rich, to raise a family, to own a stable of thoroughbreds, and to add to the glory of the Catholic Church." He would also add that he hoped there would be "a good room in Heaven waiting for me at the end."

Shortly before the death of his beloved wife, the Squire realized his dream of riches, and he did have a young family to raise. Now it was time to achieve the rest of his life plan. In 1893, he purchased 350 acres of rolling farmland in Westchester County, located about thirty miles north of New York City. The property, which he called "East View Farm," included a beautiful Victorian mansion, tennis courts, a swimming pool, as well as horse stables and a racetrack.

It was at East View that the Squire was finally able to

indulge in his lifelong love of horses and horse racing. He purchased several trotting horses, and he would ship them to races in Long Island. In 1902, he purchased land in Yonkers and built the Empire City Racetrack. Eventually realizing that there was far more money to be made in horseback racing than harness racing, he soon switched from trotters to thoroughbreds.

According to Stephen Birmingham's book, the Squire's attempts to move into New York's racing circles raised eyebrows among the members of its elite Jockey Club. The idea of a Roman Catholic Irishman joining this lofty group of blue-blooded Protestants was too much for the membership to accept. Although they tried mightily to keep the outsider from infiltrating their circles, in the end, after a three-year court battle, James Butler won, and was able to open his own racetrack, Empire City. Despite that, he was never invited to join the Jockey Club. His response toward this overt act of discrimination was simply to state, "To hell with them."

Empire City was considered to be a simple track, offering fewer social niceties than established tracks such as Belmont. But it was a racetrack built for the everyman, and it became quite popular with the working class. It was also profitable. Part of that profitability was due to the Squire's frugal spending habits that included a barebones racing venue and a penchant for buying horses in quantity.

My great-grandfather wanted to show the world that great racehorses didn't have to come from Kentucky, Virginia, or Tennessee. He believed they could be raised in New

York just as well. He began breeding his own horses and became quite good at it, producing several horses with notable winning records. Birmingham notes that between 1913 and 1933, the farm produced fourteen stake winners and Butler horses won a combined total of nearly $650,000.

James Butler eventually invested in other racetracks. He owned a significant share of Laurel Park in Maryland and invested in a track built in Juarez, Mexico. It is said he once spent a pleasant afternoon chatting with Pancho Villa. When racing was banned temporarily in some states, he reportedly invested in Mexican racetracks, becoming partners with Villa and Matt Winn, longtime president of Churchill Downs.

Though frugal, the Squire was so devoted to his horses that when the cart horses he used to deliver groceries grew too old to work, he would pay to have them shipped to East View Farm to live out their final days in comfort on the estate's green fields.

But my great-grandfather could be less than generous when it came to giving his wife household funds or his children spending money. Whenever any of them needed cash, he would instead give them tips on which horses were likely to win in the next round of races. He would personally see to it that their two-dollar bets were placed with the "right people." They usually won. According to a family story that has been passed down, some mornings at breakfast, Mrs. Butler would ask her husband, "What shall we pray for today, dear?" The Squire's answer was almost invariably, "Pray for good weather and a fast track."

★ ★ ★

Through all the years of success in his financial life and with his horses and his family, my great-grandfather always remained devout in his faith and generous in his giving to the Catholic Church. He often held parties, picnics, and other outings for Catholic orphans at East View Farms. He was famous for inviting cardinals and bishops to the estate. When Catholic dignitaries would visit, he would entertain lavishly, decorating the house with Papal and American flags and providing bountiful quantities of food and drink. Perhaps his most notable contribution to the Catholic Church was his role in co-founding with his cousin, Mother Marie Joseph Butler, the network of women's schools known as Marymount.

In 1860, five years after James Butler was born in Kilkenny, his cousin, Johanna Butler was born just a few miles away. She was the seventh child of John and Ellen Butler, who like James's parents, were farmers. In 1876, Johanna entered the religious congregation of the Sacred Heart of Mary in Beziers, France. She took the name Marie Joseph when she made her final vows in 1880. Following completion of her own education, Sr. Marie Joseph was sent to Portugal where she taught school for two decades. In 1903, she was sent as the Mother Superior to Sag Harbor, Long Island, tasked with growing the congregation's presence in the United States.

Upon his cousin's arrival, the Squire donated generously to her plans to build a school for girls. Coincidentally (or perhaps providentially), his wife Mary shortly before her death had urged him to build an academy that would educate young Catholic women. In 1907, the Squire purchased a large, old home and land in nearby Tarrytown and gifted them to the order.

Several years later, he purchased other property located on the same street to add to the growing school. In 1926, the academy became formally known as Marymount College. That same year, during a meeting of the Board of Trustees, James officially handed his cousin, now known as Mother Butler, the deed to the property. Although the college was named in honor of the Virgin Mary, James liked to believe that it was named after his late wife.

Later that year, the Squire also purchased additional land in Manhattan for a city branch of the growing college. Eventually the network would grow to more than twenty-five Marymount high schools and colleges in the US and Europe. And his generosity wasn't geared to Marymount alone. He was a significant benefactor of the Church of the Magdalene in Pocantico Hills, New York. In appreciation of his many contributions to the Catholic Church, in 1912, Pope Pius X named him a Knight Commander of the Order of Saint Gregory.

James Butler passed away in 1934 after a brief illness. He was seventy-nine years old. His funeral was held at St. Patrick's Cathedral in New York. More than 3,000 people attended the funeral. His remains were laid to rest beside his wife's remains at the family crypt at Marymount Tarrytown.

★ ★ ★

In many ways, the Squire was a simple man. He had no desire to belong to any of New York City's name-dropping, hoity-toity clubs. The one club he did join was the Andiron Club, where he would drop in to have a drink or play a round of poker. He was wealthy, but he never chose to flaunt that money.

East View Farm was located very near the Rockefeller estate. The Squire became friends with J.D. Rockefeller and occasionally the two would have a drink together. Rockefeller once asked him if he would be interested in playing a round of golf—to which the Squire is said to have scoffed, "Golf? That's a rich man's game."

When he was urged by several New York politicians to run for elected office, James refused adamantly, insisting that he was but a simple grocer and a grocer he would remain. His Irish roots ran deep.

James Butler had his faults. He was a strict parent—perhaps a bit too strict. His children reportedly regarded him with a mix of awe and dread. Some say his tough-minded parenting after the death of his wife went a little too far. His reluctance to give his children spending money—instead making them place racing bets—remained all his life. He would often say, "None of my children will be spendthrifts!" According to Birmingham's book, the

Squire left behind what some of his children considered a "tough-minded will," in which he only "gave each child $100,000 at age twenty-five, $125,000 at age thirty, and the balance of the inheritance at age thirty-five, minus $250,000 that was set aside in an unshatterable trust."

As I look at my great-grandfather's life, it strikes me what an interesting example he is of life in those times. I have learned a lot from studying him. What is becoming clearer to me is an awareness of how the Squire was able to focus on those four areas of his life that mattered deeply to him: He loved horses; he loved his family; he loved his business; and the spiritual side was very important to him.

Both my great-grandfather and his cousin, Mother Butler, set the stage for spirituality in our family. Their Catholic faith has been handed down through the generations. The Squire's son (my grandfather) and my father regularly attended church on Sundays, as I did and still do. Contributing to charities associated with the Church was important.

Overall, the family has remained involved with the Church. Perhaps in my own generation, our level of spirituality has decreased a bit. I sense that perhaps material values have gained more importance.

As time has gone on, there are aspects of our faith and its rules that some in the family have had difficulty complying with. The moral values have slipped a little bit. Maybe it's become easier to feel a little less guilty about failings. Less guilt can be good, but it also can make us more willing to bend the rules in our own favor.

With ensuing generations, education has grown in importance. While I'm not certain if Grandfather Butler went to college, it was clear that he insisted his children all have good educations. His son, my father, also felt that way. He sent his children to private schools, boarding schools, and good colleges.

And so, as I review the Squire's life, I can't help but wonder about future generations: What are their values going to be? What set of standards will they have? What changes will there be? How will the values that we currently have help us cope with that?

As it happens, my paternal great-grandfather was not my only ancestor with the golden touch with money. My maternal grandfather had it too.

CHAPTER 3

WILLIAM "PA" EWING

MY MATERNAL GRANDFATHER, WILLIAM EWING, WAS born in St. Louis, Missouri on July 27, 1880, to Frederick and Jessie (Valle) Ewing. Frederick, who died in 1897, had held a successful job with the Missouri Glass Company before becoming a cattleman with a group in San Angelo, Texas.

Grandfather, whom we called "Pa," had grown up with one brother and one sister. Although not much is known about his childhood, he appears to have spent an extended amount of time in Europe with his mother. He was seventeen when his father died. He attended the Sheffield Scientific School at Yale University and graduated in 1903.

Upon graduation, he began his working career as a rodman with CB&Q Railroad. In an update William submitted to the Yale Club for a triennial class reunion book, he noted that the job entailed a move from Chicago to Lacrosse,

Wisconsin. While with the railroad, he rose to the position of first assistant for the entire Chicago division.

He left CB&Q in 1906 and started with the Chicago-based Northwest Harrison Company working in the bond business. According to his obituary in *The New York Times*, in 1916, he joined the staff of banking leviathan, J.P. Morgan and Company that year and became a partner in 1927. He resigned with several other employees in 1935 to create Morgan Stanley & Company. He served as executive vice president of the firm and was named a limited partner in 1941.

He was with J.P. Morgan when, on September 16, 1920, just as the lunch rush was beginning, a heavily loaded horse-drawn cart stopped in front of the US Assay Office and directly across the street from the J.P. Morgan building on Wall Street. The driver exited the cart and walked away quickly, melting into the crowds on the street, and never to be seen again. At 12:01 p.m., the cart exploded, sending metal fragments and shrapnel across the crowded street.

The horrific destruction extended outward in a half-mile radius. More than thirty people were killed and well over 300 injured. The explosion blew out the window of several buildings, including the New York Stock Exchange and the J.P. Morgan offices. Like many others, stockbroker Joseph P. Kennedy, the father of the future President John F. Kennedy was lifted several inches off his feet by the force of the concussion. The sound of the explosion was earsplitting. A block away, a streetcar was knocked off its rails by the blast.

J.P. Morgan employee Andrew Dunn later told the FBI, "It was enough to knock you out by itself." Inside the Morgan building, the entire office was covered in broken glass, scattered papers, and twisted remains of steel wire screens. Multiple guests and employees of the firm were seriously injured. One Morgan employee was dead, and a second one succumbed to his injuries a day later. My grandfather did not escape unscathed. He was knocked unconscious and awoke several minutes later to find his head wedged in a wastebasket.

To this day, responsibility for the blast has never been determined. The FBI, the New York Police and Fire Departments, and the US Secret Service all pursued leads for years. Hundreds of people were interviewed and investigated but few could give the authorities any information that was helpful. No one could give a definitive description of what the driver looked like. It is believed that the perpetrators were a small group of anti-capitalist Italian anarchists.

But in the end, if the goal of the bombing was to cripple Wall Street's operations, it had little impact. The day after the bombing, windows were boarded and many workers wore bandages, but offices and banks were open for business.

Unlike my great-grandfather Butler, William Ewing was a joiner. He belonged to several clubs including the Book and Snake Society at Yale. He was a member of the Yale University Club, The Links, The Jockey Club, and the Goldens Bridge Hounds. He served as a trustee for the North Westchester Hospital Association.

Pa married Maria Taylor in 1910. She was considered to be the second most beautiful woman in all of St. Louis. (How she came by the title of second most beautiful was never explained in the family lore.) They had four children: William, Jane, Jessie Valle, and Grace Valle. Jessie was my mother. In later years, William and Marie moved to Mount Kisco, New York.

Even after my grandmother died, Pa continued to live in the Mount Kisco home. I remember it well. It was lovely and quite large with at least five bedrooms. There was a live-in staff of three. Pa had a wine cellar built into the rise of a small hill on the property. Pa owned several acres of land as well as a stable of thoroughbreds and a practice racetrack. He had a full-time overseer to look after the stables and horses.

Several times Pa hosted Thanksgiving dinners for the entire Ewing clan. By then, his children had married, and he had twenty-one grandchildren. His son William (I knew him as Uncle Bill, of course) had nine children, my Aunt Grace had eight children, and my mother had four children including me.

Pa's wife was lovely. Her nickname was "Gogo." She was quiet and a bit removed but very nice. She had obviously been a beautiful woman in her youth, so her title from her St. Louis days made sense. Gogo died at Mount Kisco in March 1957 at age seventy-two.

Every year in the summer, Pa would rent a house in Quissett Harbor, Massachusetts, which is located between

Falmouth and Woods Hole on Cape Cod, for July and August. The house would be available for his children and grandchildren to use. My Aunt Gracie would usually get there in July and Mom's turn was in August.

Pa was the type of person who you'd say hello and exchange pleasantries with but as a grandchild, I would never have sat down with him and gotten into a long conversation. He was an old-style grandparent, and such familiarity didn't happen. We were very polite and respectful to him. He would send us presents at Christmas and birthdays and special occasions. We would always send thank-you notes. I don't remember him as stern, but the relationship between grandparents and grandchildren was definitely more formal than it is today.

However, according to family reputation, he was quite strict with his children, although I have only heard one specific story that would seem to verify that. It involved my mother. She had apparently gotten home quite late from a date. When she came into the house, Pa met her at the top of the stairs, and he asked what was going on. She started arguing with him and, according to Mom, she wound up at the bottom of the staircase.

He had a strong personality. He was a hard worker. Once he made up his mind, that was that. He stuck with his decision. And he was exceptionally physically fit. Even in his seventies, when we were at Cape Cod, he would swim every day from the shore to a raft some distance out and back in again. He set a good example for all of us. He had a commanding presence and that carried over to the next generation.

His only son, my Uncle Bill, was a good steward of all that Pa passed on to him. He was careful with the trusts that he was responsible for handling after Pa died. When someone needed some extra money for unexpected expenses, Uncle Bill would step in and help them out. When I was in the hospital after my accident, he visited me. He and the trustees found the very best lawyers to handle my case against the owners of the buoy.

His daughters also seemed to display his sense of responsibility and resolution. If one of her own children wasn't following the rules, and Mom was especially exasperated, she would occasionally drop a comment such as, "Oh, grow up."

My Aunt Jane also had a mind of her own. She was a lovely lady and had done some photo shoots and modeling for Vogue or one of those other fancy magazines. She was athletic—a good skier and horseback rider. After my Uncle Bill was sent to Arizona because of his asthma, as the next oldest, she sort of took his place. When she decided what she wanted to do, she went ahead and did it. She was married four times.

My Aunt Grace had a very spiritual side. She was very thoughtful and spent a lot of time exploring her more artistic inclinations. I think that may have been hard on her husband and children when she was deep in concentration. She did divorce her husband, Uncle Moore at one point, but took him back when he became ill, although they never remarried.

★ ★ ★

Like the Squire, Pa Ewing was very much into horse racing. While he never owned or invested in racetracks, he did have stables and a practice track for thoroughbreds that he entered in races. A chance encounter between the Butler and Ewing families did once happen at a racetrack. The course at the Aqueduct track in Jamaica, New York, had just been redone. My father was the head of renovation for the track. On the opening day of the new racetrack, Pa Ewing had a horse running in the seventh race. The seventh race is usually the biggest event of a racing day at almost all tracks. It's where the best horses are run and the largest amount of money is bet.

My dad, of course, was there and all of us kids were invited. We all went up to the upper tier to watch a horse that Pa Ewing had running in the seventh race. The horse won the race. So, it happened that a Ewing had a horse win a race run on a track that a Butler was responsible for building.

Somewhere, there is a family photo of Pa being presented the trophy by then-Governor Nelson Rockefeller. So, it's interesting that both sides of the family were into horse racing, and both once shared a track for one day.

Like everyone, Pa had his quirks and did not adjust to the times in every respect. Despite all his accomplishments, he never seemed fully comfortable driving an automobile.

Grandfather Ewing was a man of careful planning and great foresight. Not too long before his death, he set up trusts for the children and divided up his holdings in a fair and equitable manner. He wanted to set up trusts that would be protected for generations. Those irrevocable trusts were set up with the help of one of New York's top legal firms. Disbursements were to be paid annually to his children while they were living and then the grandchildren. The principle of the trust, which has never been touched, continues to grow until the income beneficiary dies and the principle is equally distributed to the next generation. The distributed principle is not subject to federal income taxes.

His actions and thoughtful preparations had an impact on me. Thanks to his example, I learned to think about and plan for my own future generations. Following in Pa's footsteps, I have set up living trusts for my children.

Pa Ewing lived a full life. He died at age eighty-four at St. Luke's Hospital on May 19, 1965. But there is much more to the Ewing family story and the legacy Pa left behind. We shall return to the topic in a later chapter.

CHAPTER 4

JAMES BUTLER JR. AND JAMES BUTLER III

THE SQUIRE'S OLDEST SON, JAMES BUTLER II, WAS MY grandfather. As a young man, he followed his father into the grocery business; he also shared his father's love of horses. His true passion was thoroughbred racing.

Although he met with some success early, his would not be a long life, and problems with drink plagued him. He was born in 1891 and grew up spending time between the family estate, East View, and New York City. Like the Squire, he never attended college, but seemed to have learned the business through on-the-job training and experience. He was also reported to be a gifted writer.

Just as my grandfather took control of his father's stores in 1935, the grocery world was changing. James Butler Groceries filed for bankruptcy in 1938, and was subsequently bought out by the well-known A&P grocery chain.

So, James II threw himself into managing the family's racing interests. He served as president of the Empire Racetrack for years. After the Squire's death, he immediately set about upgrading the facility to bring it on par with other New York tracks. He also improved the Laurel Park track in Maryland. His renovations were so well done that they immediately drew the attention of racing experts across the state. He became an outstanding figure in the world of racing, and his expertise was often called upon in consultations and inspections when other courses were being upgraded.

Unlike his father, my grandfather moved comfortably in New York's top racing circles. It is notable that he was a member of the New York Jockey Club—the same organization that the Squire was never invited to join.

In July 1915, James Butler II married a former New York City debutante, Dorothy Clair Conron. Their wedding took place at St. Patrick's Cathedral in New York City. It was quite the social event. The reception was held at the Hotel St. Regis. The couple had three children: Dorothy, Pierce, and my father, James Jr., who was born in January 1918.

Unfortunately, James Butler II died in October 1940, nearly two years before I was born. His early death at the age of forty-nine was the result of a horseback-riding incident. He was thrown from his saddle when his horse caught its hoof going over a jump. Grandfather's neck was broken, and he is said to have died instantly. Prior to his death he had been sharing a leisurely lunch with his wife and then decided to go for the fatal ride.

It was said that James had problems with alcoholism. Unfortunately, due to his early death, and then my father's own early death, I was never able to gather many personal details about him. James Butler II's wife, my Grandma Dottie, remarried twice and passed away in November of 1991.

★ ★ ★

James's and Dorothy's oldest son was James Butler III. My father grew up in a very good world—one that was both spiritually and materially rich.

He loved life, somewhat in the manner of a raconteur. Dad was very active in the New York sports world and social scene. He was quite popular. While at Yale, he was captain of the rugby team and served as the manager of the university's football team—which was actually quite good at the time.

In the spring of 1941, my father's senior year and just before his graduation, the rugby team went to the Bahamas to play a local team down there. Much to their surprise, the Yale Bulldogs lost several matches, quite badly. They were so surprised by the losses, they decided to remain in the Bahamas and keep practicing. As a result, they overstayed their departure date.

Dad was in an Honors English class and his senior thesis had to be completed before he could graduate. Because he was still playing rugby in the Caribbean, he didn't get it in by the deadline. His professor called him and informed him that as a result, he would not be able to graduate. The professor offered him the chance to submit the paper in the fall semester and graduate then. My dad thought about it for a bit, but said, "No, thank you. All my friends are leaving, and I don't want to stay around." So, he just left and never did officially graduate from Yale, despite completing the major amount of the necessary work. He opted to go straight into the business world.

Like his grandfather and father before him, Dad loved the racing scene. He served as president of the Empire City Racing Association from 1946 to 1953, secretary of the Thoroughbred Association from 1947 to 1953, and later as a director of the New York Racing Association.

He had married my mother, Jessie Valle Ewing, on May 3, 1941, at Saint Patrick's Church in Bedford, New York. Growing up, they had both loved horses and ridden together in the Golden Bridge Hunt. Seven months after they were married, Pearl Harbor was bombed. Like most healthy young men, my father joined the military.

Dad enlisted in the US Army Air Force in 1942. He initially hoped to become a pilot, but his vision wasn't good enough. When that fell through, he wanted to become a navigator, and that meant undergoing another physical exam. A couple of friends took Dad out the night before, apparently in a misguided attempt to bring his blood pressure down or to address some other physical issue. The plan did not seem to have worked, but Dad eventually joined the Air Force as a navigator.

During his time in the war, Dad was stationed with the Military Air Transport Command. They were responsible for delivering bombers to ally and US bases. While I didn't hear many stories, I do know that often they'd fly from London or other European cities into Marrakech, North Africa, and other exciting places. They'd be there for a day or two and visit all the local bars. The bomber crews, which included the movie star Bruce Cabot, all became good friends.

After the war ended, Dad started looking after things in the family racing business. He was also involved in a lot of other sporting activities. It seems he knew everyone who was anyone in the sporting world, from the great sportscaster, Red Barber, to the Four Horsemen of Notre Dame, as well as some of the greatest boxers of the era.

When we lived in Old Westbury, Long Island, Dad would take the train into New York City to his Empire City offices near Grand Central Station. He did that for a while, but it became a problem over time. It seems some of the members of the upper-class racing circles began to think that Empire City was taking too much business away from other tracks, such as Jamaica, Aqueduct, and Saratoga.

The owners of those tracks worked to establish the New York Racing Association, a nonprofit organization that began to set racing dates for all the racecourses in the state. The organization began taking more and more dates from Empire City and awarding them to others. As a result, there were fewer racing days, fewer races, and fewer bets to place at Empire City. People stopped coming. Eventually, there was no longer enough revenue coming in to cover maintenance, personnel, and stable costs. This became a real problem for my father. The family eventually had to sell Empire City and Dad went into the real estate business. I think he began drinking more heavily at that time.

Dad's alcohol consumption started to become a problem with my parents. There had been happy times in the family, as my mom and dad enjoyed time with me and my siblings and watching us grow. But as my dad's drinking seemed to get worse, it was destroying the marriage. They began arguing and that escalated to the point that they divorced in 1960, just before I went off to college at Yale. They were both Roman Catholic, and divorcing was quite difficult in those days. The complications and resulting long time span resulted in Mom obtaining a civil divorce.

Both ended up remarrying. My mother married a very nice man named Lou who was our landscaper. She had known him for a while. He was also a fine sailor; Mom was fond of the water. It ended up being a wonderful marriage.

In the meantime, Dad had met a very attractive woman, Carolyn MacLeod, during a visit to Martha's Vineyard. She and dad would marry less than a month after Mom got remarried.

Despite his drinking, Dad and I usually got along reasonably well. But the night of my twenty-first birthday, it created conflict between us.

This was the fall of 1964, and I was preparing to enter my senior year. I had just returned from a summer spent working for my Uncle Louis overseas in Columbia. My dad called and said, "Let's celebrate your twenty-first birthday." His drinking had reached a point that I remember thinking to myself at the time, "Oh geez, please don't drink too much." But off we went, and we were fine—until we got back to his apartment. When we got there, he continued to drink. At one point, he fell and I knew he was very drunk.

I leaned over and asked in a sort of snide, twenty-one-year-old way, "Dad, can I help you up?"

He just looked at me and said, "Get out of my apartment."

I left him, but I didn't know what I was going to do. It was midnight, I was in New York City, and I only had a bit of money on me. I didn't have credit cards or anything else at the time. I called up one of Dad's relatives and said, "I'm sorry to bother you, Uncle Walter, but Dad's had a problem. I think he's not too well or had too much to drink. He fell and then he threw me out, and he locked his apartment. I'm worried about him. Could you get somebody to check him?"

Uncle Walter went over and looked after him and everything worked out. But after that, Dad and I were put off with each other for a time. Thank God, we eventually patched things up, and in later years, before I was sent overseas for a work assignment, Margot and I would play tennis with him and my stepmother, Carolyn.

I'm thankful we did grow close again, because years later, when I was working in Central America, I got word that my dad had died suddenly from a heart attack. This was July 1969, one of the most eventful months—both terrible and wonderful—of my life.

That month, war had broken out in Central America between El Salvador and Honduras. Margot was pregnant at the time, and our first son—the fifth James Butler (I, of course, being the fourth James Butler)—was born there.

I got word to family in the states, including my dad. James Butler III received the news via telegraph that James Butler V had been born. Two weeks later dad died, having never met his grandson. Dad was fifty-one.

The news was crushing, of course, and there was also the practical matter of getting to his funeral. Asking Margot and an infant to travel internationally at the time was not realistic, but I also needed to be at my dad's funeral. I managed to make it home in time, briefly join the family in mourning, and return to San Salvador, which was then at war. That most memorable month was capped by the first moon landing at the end of July 1969.

★ ★ ★

Both my grandfather and my father died too early, at forty-nine and fifty-one respectively. Both men also suffered from the curse of alcoholism. As a younger man, and Irish, I often thought about their untimely deaths and wondered if being the fourth James Butler in the line, I would perhaps be subject to the same fate. In addition to the fame and fortune that my father and his father before him had passed on to me, would I also inherit these two curses?

I was fortunate to never have an attraction to drinking excessively. But I did experience a far too-close call with death in my early fifties. I could easily have died in the boating accident on Long Island Sound. I am thankful that I did survive, and as a result I developed a greater appreciation for life and for the opportunity to live my faith on a more spiritually active level.

CHAPTER 5

MY MOM, JESSIE EWING

MY MOTHER WAS PA EWING'S MIDDLE DAUGHTER. SHE had an older brother, an older sister, and one younger sister. I think that the burden of the family's social expectations fell more on her older siblings, making my mom a bit more independent minded and sometimes stubborn.

Pa was strict with his children, but he clearly loved them very much and looked out for them. When my mother was preparing to marry my father, he gave her the chance to call off the wedding.

This was after the invitations had all gone out and everything had been arranged. It would have been socially awkward, and I am sure somewhat costly. But nonetheless he gave her the option. He pulled her aside and said to her, "Jessie, if you don't want to do this, just tell me."

Pa Ewing had already been through three weddings with his other children. While my parents probably loved each other very much when they married, I think my grandfather might have suspected my father's weaknesses, or perhaps he just subconsciously knew there were going to be future problems.

Whatever the reason, it's apparent that Pa Ewing was worried about his daughter. That's just an example of how prescient he was in looking out for the long-term happiness and well-being of all his children.

As someone who was immersed in the world of finances, my mother's father also took great care to provide for the financial security of his children after he was gone. He believed it was important to pass his wealth on to his family in a responsible manner. Around 1957, he set up irrevocable trust funds for each of his children: Bill, Jane, Jessie, and Grace. He continued to add assets to those trusts over the years.

Thanks to Pa Ewing's provisions, my mother, her sisters and brother continued to receive a monthly income after he passed away. After Mom and her siblings all passed away, their children—myself, my sisters and brother, as well as my cousins, have continued to receive distributions. Pa had also arranged irrevocable trusts for his grandchildren whereby they would receive income and upon their death, the principal would be shared within the next generation.

Because of his background, Pa Ewing showed more foresight in providing for ensuing generations than the Butlers did. While the Squire left some money to his children, the great wealth he accumulated wasn't passed down equally and most disappeared within two generations.

James Butler was reportedly worth about $30 million when he died, but his "tough-minded" will awarded each child only $100,000 at age twenty-five, another $125,000 at age thirty, and the balance of the inheritance was awarded each child when they reached thirty-five, minus $250,000 that was set aside in trust.

Upon the Squire's death in 1934, my grandfather became president of the grocery store chain. He had difficulty running the business and was ill-prepared to steer the stores successfully through the turbulence of the Great Depression. Within just a few years, the company was forced to reorganize and file for bankruptcy.

There wasn't a great deal of money to pass down, and because my father died before my grandmother, she gained control of the Butler money. Apparently, Grammie Dottie rewrote her will several times. Dad had been completely written out of the will years before she died. At the time, her estate had been worth about $2 million but my father and his children received none of it.

In comparison, William Ewing Jr, tried to be as fair as possible in equally providing for each of his children. The only exception to this were two properties he owned in Maryland and Bermuda that he left to my Uncle Bill, his son.

After Pa Ewing's death, Uncle Bill also took on management of the Ewing family financial interests. Like his father before him, he has handled that responsibility quite well.

All of this impacted my mother's life for the better, while what happened to the Butler family fortune was to my father's detriment. The Ewing concern for the next generation's financial security was a lesson Margot and I took to heart. We have set up funds for our own children.

★ ★ ★

Although my mother grew up quite wealthy, she never flaunted it. She didn't really involve herself in most of New York's whirlwind of social events and extravagant parties that were going on. She didn't have to have a gorgeous dress or stunning new pin for every affair.

Dad bought her a lovely engagement ring but overall, she wasn't really into material things that much. She did have some good jewels that she kept in a lockbox. After she died, some of the jewelry in her safety deposit boxes somehow went missing.

Maybe her lack of interest in high society was because my mom was a third child and as such wasn't raised with all the expectations of the older children. Her role as the little sister turned her into more of a caregiver to her mother than her siblings.

She did enjoy having servants in the house and staff to maintain the lawns and gardens of the estate. She always insisted we look nice when we left the house or had people visiting. When I left for boarding school, she gave me reassuring words and made sure that I had all the right clothes.

Mom cared for her children very much. She was especially anxious about our health—both physical and mental. This may have been because of her brother Bill's health issues when she was growing up. He, like me, suffered from severe asthma as a child.

Her fears around this is why Mom sent me to Arizona as an infant and Florida as a child when I developed serious asthma, although it was also recommended to her as the right thing to do.

Perhaps in the case of my younger brother, Ewing, she may have been overprotective of his health issues. He had suffered from epilepsy since he was about nine or ten. The kids on his school bus would make fun of him and she tried to change that by changing schools. I don't think her hovering concern was fully positive for him. He had trouble learning to handle life on his own. His approaches to life did adjust after his marriages and our mother's death.

Of course, like all mothers, she wasn't always happy with our behavior. There were times she wasn't particularly happy with my sister, Dorothy, who could be obnoxious or rebellious at times to her teachers. It reached the point where she was pulled out of Mount St. Vincent Academy, where she was boarding because the nuns there sent her home. Dottie did make some adjustments and returned to graduate from the Academy.

I think seeing my dad struggle was very frustrating for my mom to watch. Dad was having a rough go of things. He was in financial trouble with the real estate firm he was managing, and he had recently dealt with the devastating loss of the racetrack. He was arguing with other family members and drinking more heavily. And he was seeing other women.

I think the financial problems and business struggles Dad was experiencing compounded his drinking and other issues. It had to be difficult for him as the father figure to accept that it was Mom's money that was keeping the family afloat. It was Mom's money that sent me to college and most likely Mom's resources that provided for a registered nurse to take me to Florida when I was young. Dad contributed to the family income with the daily food supply and paying the servants' salaries, but Mom covered most of the expenses.

At one point, around 1958, my mother called him out about a woman he was seeing on a semi-regular basis. She also talked to her own father about what she should do. He asked her if she had ever thought about getting a divorce and offered to help her with that. She thought about it but held on for another year or so.

After my parents did get divorced, Mom continued to be the one who ran things. Right through her eighties, she was still talking to us, giving advice, issuing orders, and sending us money if and when we needed it.

As I was growing up, I think I was more impressed by

my mom's values than my father's. Like her, I was never into flagrant displays of wealth. I don't drive a Cadillac or wear particularly expensive shirts and coats like my father. He certainly had a flair for that sort of thing. And while growing up, I never thought about going into the Butler family business, the racetracks, or any of those ventures. I went to the other side of the family and became involved in banking. The seeds for that future were planted during the 1940s and 1950s, when I grew up in a different America than today.

James Butler

William Ewing

James Butler store in the 1920s

J.P. Morgan Bank 23 Wall Street

James Butler Jr. and Jessie Valle Ewing, 1941 wedding

CHAPTER 6

AN AMERICAN CHILDHOOD IN THE '40S AND '50S

I WAS SIX MONTHS OLD WHEN I CAME DOWN WITH A serious case of double pneumonia. It was about that time when my doctors also realized that I suffered from asthma—which was a dangerous condition to suffer from in a cold Northern climate like New York state. The disease may have run in the family, as my mother's brother had suffered from it as a child many years earlier.

The doctors recommended my parents send me somewhere to a warmer climate. I was sent to Arizona around my first birthday. Arizona is where my earliest childhood memories come from; no more than three years old and sleeping in a crib in a bright room. Some of my earliest and fondest recollections from those early years are with the warm and caring registered nurse my parents had hired to stay with me in Arizona. Her name was Evangeline Canning Fogarty, but to me, she was simply Aunt Vange.

The two of us, myself and Aunt Vange, stayed out west for two years before I was able to return to my parents' home in Mount Kisco, New York, a small town in the Western district of the state. I attended preschool at Mrs. Stoddard's School for Little People. While I was there—I was probably age five or six—I remained fairly healthy. I enjoyed the school and thought it was good fun in that world. But it was during that time when my parents decided to move to Old Westbury, a small township located on Long Island, New York.

A friend of my dad's lived there, and that family had seized on an opportunity to buy a nicer house. With my dad's financial struggles, it was my mom who actually purchased the house with the help of her family. In Westbury, I attended school for a couple years at Greenvale School, located on Long Island. But by second grade, I was frequently getting sick again. Having a lot of breathing issues, I ended up spending most of the school year in bed.

Because of my absences, the school felt I wasn't ready to graduate to the third grade, so my parents once again got in touch with the registered nurse, Aunt Vange. This time, the two of us were sent to Fort Lauderdale, Florida. I was admitted to a school called Pine Crest and I was there for four years—from second through sixth grade.

I think I became a lifelong reader because of my childhood asthma. There was time for a lot of reading. Being confined to a bed, I was well-read enough that when I first started Pine Crest, the educators there initially thought I would be able to enter the third grade, because it looked as if I had a well-rounded education. Unfortunately, that didn't prove to be the case and I was placed back in second grade. For the rest of my school years, I was a year behind other kids my age.

Aunt Vange was like a second mom to me, and I believe many of my values later in life were shaped by my experiences with her. When we first moved down to Fort Lauderdale, I was struck by where we were going to be living. It was far different from my family's Georgian brick home on Long Island. Our temporary home was a two-story apartment building with three apartments on each level. It was located off Broward Boulevard in Fort Lauderdale. It was only about three or four blocks away from my school, so most days I usually walked or rode a bike to get there.

The landlord who managed the apartment building, Mrs. Hanks, had a daughter and a son. The son, Roger, was my age. I played with him fairly often, but he went to public school. My school, Pine Crest, was private. Despite that difference, we had fun together. In a lot of things we did, there was a bit of good-natured rivalry.

Aunt Vange and I lived in a second-floor apartment, which had two bedrooms, a bathroom, a kitchen, a small dining area, and living room. We had a television in the living room, and I remember often sitting and watching it together, and often laughing along with whatever program was on.

Aunt Vange was in her mid-fifties. She was about five feet, three inches tall. She had dark hair with a bit of gray. She had a quiet personality, but she could certainly make herself heard if she wanted to. She had a good sense of humor. Not only was she a registered nurse, but she also did the cooking and cleaned the apartment. She took good care of me, going beyond what might normally be expected from a paid caregiver.

My mother told me that Aunt Vange had done something very similar for one of the big-name newspaper families. It was perhaps the Pulitzers but I can't be sure of that. She had cared for a boy who was probably five or ten years older than I was. She was very familiar with this particular type of caregiving.

When I was first told I needed to go to Florida, I was surprised to learn I'd be moving out of the house and going to live with somebody else. But when I met Aunt Vange again, I was reassured, and Mom also made sure I knew that I would be coming back home in the summer. She also promised that we would stay in touch, and we did write back and forth. So, my initial worries didn't last very long and soon disappeared completely.

I required the care of a registered nurse like Aunt Vange because of the asthma and severe allergies that I suffered from. Those health concerns also caused skin problems and other issues. My allergies were related to different types of pollen, to fish, to animals, and to dairy products. I was on a strict diet until I was about thirteen years old. If I had cereal, it was with something other than regular milk. I didn't have ice cream until I was thirteen years old. I was always conscious of the fact that if I wanted to stay healthy, I had to follow strict guidelines.

Aunt Vange made sure I was involved in lots of after-school activities and helped me make friends. In addition to Roger, she would ask me about friends at school and encourage me to play with them.

She and I would do things occasionally on the weekend. Sometimes, we would take a bus into town or go to a movie. Back then, movie theaters would feature two cartoons and a serial before the main feature. She was nice enough to take the extra time to go with me to watch the cartoons along with the main feature.

I don't know if she got me interested in delivering newspapers or I decided I wanted to do it myself, but I'd seen an ad on TV looking for boys who could deliver the paper while riding a bicycle. For a time, I delivered the Fort Lauderdale newspaper by throwing the paper from my bicycle. My route was only a few blocks, and I kept it for a couple of years.

Aunt Vange always made sure I finished my homework, the start of a good habit. With her help, I became interested in several classes that hadn't interested me before. Mathematics was one of those. She helped me realize the challenge in subjects like math and science.

She was a deeply devout Catholic. She was there when I received the sacrament of Confirmation. We went to church every Sunday and she made sure that I got to confession frequently. She was very involved in the Church. Catholicism had always been a strong thread running through many generations in my family, and Aunt Vange played a key role in introducing me to my faith.

I also learned about the value of dedication while living in Florida with her. It's a word that has come to mean a lot to me. It's important to be dedicated to something. There were times when I wasn't totally successful in being dedicated. Those were times I should have, to use an expression from those days, "cut the cards sooner."

She also helped me develop other interests. One of those outside hobbies was a riflery program offered by the National Rifle Association. Back then, the organization was not super political and offered lessons and target range shooting. The instructors would teach you to compete and earn proficiency badges. You started off as a Pro Marksman and worked your way up to Distinguished Rifleman. I earned my third bar as a sharpshooter and aimed at getting to Distinguished Rifleman.

There was a kind gentleman who would come pick me up and take me to the range. That's when I got my own rifle, a Mossberg 22. I kept it at the range. I enjoyed that sport very much. At one point, though, I did make a mistake.

One day, we were shooting at the range and the instructor told everyone to stop firing and mark our targets. There were people walking to the other side of the targets to measure our marks. After the instructor said to stop firing,

I still had one bullet left. I fired it. Thankfully, it went in the target, and nobody was hurt but they were not happy with me. I was not allowed to come back for a couple of weeks. After my suspension, though, I was able to continue working toward my badges. Both the penalty and realization of what might have happened were sobering.

While I was in Florida, I joined the Cub Scouts through my class at school. I enjoyed the meetings and in the sixth grade, I became a Boy Scout. We were fortunate to have good Scout leaders, although I do remember being torn and wanting to also go back to my Cub Scout group too, because I had enjoyed that as well.

Sixth grade was the last year of elementary school and my last year in Florida. Pine Crest School had safety patrols— boys with safety patrol belts who would ensure students crossed the street at the right place. The safety patrol was responsible for monitoring a couple of blocks around the school. There were between ten or fifteen students on the patrol, and I wanted to be in the program. I joined it and was appointed captain, wearing a special blue badge. I had a lieutenant; he wore a red badge and everybody else on the patrol wore a regular badge. We would come in a little early for school and stay a little later. Once a week, we would gather around the flagpole, raise the flag in the morning and say the Pledge of Allegiance.

In the spring of my sixth-grade year, the association of school safety patrols (the exact name escapes my memory) arranged for a national school safety patrol convention in Washington, DC. Kids from all over the county went to

Washington, and we participated in a march and all sorts of other activities. I went up in a train with several guys from my school and from other schools in Florida. We stayed in a nice hotel in Washington. It was quite an enjoyable experience at that age.

That year I was also elected vice president of the class but I was disappointed that I wasn't elected president. The class had elected a girl as president, which, at that time, I couldn't understand.

My parents came to visit me once while I was in Florida and I did go home to Long Island every summer from June through the end of August. I would see my two sisters and my little brother, who is eleven years younger than me (and conceived and born while I was in Fort Lauderdale).

After my sixth-grade school year, I returned to Long Island for the summer, expecting to return to Florida once again in the fall. But my parents said they had found a boarding school in Scottsdale, Arizona called the Judson School for Boys. My doctor agreed that Arizona was a good option. Mom and Dad assured me the school would take great care of me and they thought it was essential for my health. I was pretty unhappy about it, as I had become used to Florida with Aunt Vange.

When I was told that Aunt Vange wouldn't be coming back and I should say goodbye to her, that was hard to accept. It was a sad time for me for a while. Sixth grade in Florida was the last I saw of Aunt Vange for many years. I spoke to her on the phone once and wrote her a couple of letters.

But it wasn't until after I married and my son was born that my wife, Margot, suggested we take the baby to visit Aunt Vange. We were back in New York for a vacation and were able to contact her. She lived in Flushing, New York. She seemed very happy to see us and the baby. That was the last time I saw her. She died within a year of that visit.

★ ★ ★

So after my summer was over, it was time to go to the school in Arizona for the beginning of seventh grade. Dad took me out on a plane to Tucson, Arizona back in 1955. The two of us flew out to Phoenix and then drove to Scottsdale, a suburb of Phoenix, where The Judson School for Boys was located.

Before leaving me at school, we stayed at a hotel for a day or two. Dad took me out and bought me some Western-style clothes, cowboy boots, blue jeans, a couple of shirts, and a cowboy hat. He bought all of that to help me feel like I would fit in.

At the time, Judson School for Boys focused on helping kids with difficulties, whether those were physical, mental, or even personality issues. It wasn't a school where all the teachers had their master's degrees in history or math, which was the case at some high-end boarding schools. The classes were all fairly small. There were about twelve students in my seventh-grade class. Because the school was so small, faculty and students all knew each other pretty well.

It was an adjustment from Florida. I remember noticing

the difference in the kinds of heat, with Arizona of course having that desert air. I also remember thinking there were no palm trees, something I had become used to in Florida.

We had teachers in our dorm rooms, although there weren't many of us boarding—only about sixteen students from the entire school. We had a house mother who took care of us.

I learned to focus on new things because both the schoolwork and the environment were so different. Scottsdale was nothing like Fort Lauderdale. Back then, Scottsdale still had wooden boardwalks. The school had a polo field where the twelfth graders played polo. Sometimes local high school kids would drive their cars across the field to rough it up. We had one teacher who kind of watched us at night and carried a .38 pistol. It was certainly different there. I felt a bit out of place.

There was one guy in my class who was a bully and I had trouble with him. He was spouting nasty language and pushing me around. He wasn't hitting, but his aggressive attitude was triggering asthma attacks as I would become concerned.

I talked to one of the teachers who told me he understood. He explained that the normal way they handled that sort of issue at Judson was by working it out between the two in a boxing match. The teacher offered to be the referee and set up a ring for the match. We went in for three rounds. The school had boxing gloves that we wore, but it didn't have any headgear.

I went in the ring, and my asthma attack started right away. My opponent hit a lot harder than I did. I made it through three rounds, but by the end of the third round, I was really having trouble breathing. So, the teacher said, "That's it, end of match. You guys both punched pretty well, so I'm going to call this a draw."

The other guy had obviously hit me a lot more and he wasn't happy with the draw. But after that, he did treat me differently. He no longer bullied me. While this solution was mighty unconventional by today's standards, I will say that it seemed to have worked.

With that issue solved, I wanted to get involved in extracurricular activities again. I joined the Boy Scout troop that the school had started a few years before. The bully, previously mentioned, was the senior Scout in the group. He was a First-Class Scout. But by that time, I had earned the rank of Life Scout, the last rank before Eagle Scout, so I talked to the scout leader.

Sometimes you have to stand up for yourself. I said, "Wait a minute. I've been involved. I've done this, this, and this, and I really think I should be in that position." And the Scout leader decided to give me a test that I had to pass to become the leader. I'm not sure I passed with flying colors, but I apparently did enough that the teacher gave me the credit. I became the Senior Patrol Leader. That helped me enjoy being there a little bit more, and I certainly liked my time with the Boy Scouts.

There was something else I loved about Arizona. I discovered that I was not allergic to horses like I had been in the past, maybe because of the quality of the air out there. Up to that point in my life, I had allergies to animals. That was kind of tough for my mom because she loved dogs. When I was home, it was hard for her to have dogs around. But my allergies didn't bother me as much in Scottsdale, so I could enjoy horseback riding.

At home, my two sisters had learned to ride English Style like my parents. In Arizona, I learned to ride Western with the big saddles and cowboy boots. While I was there, I actually went on some fairly long rides. Once, I remember spending the night in a tent in the desert.

After Judson, I never really continued horseback riding. But like most kids back then, I had seen all the Western movies, and while I was in Arizona, I found I could now identify with the silent cowboy types when I was in the saddle.

The other thing the school offered was popular operas like Gilbert and Sullivan. The twelfth-grade students would put the play on. I was in the seventh grade so there really wasn't a part for me. But the faculty let me turn the pages for the teacher who played piano during the play. Not exactly a starring role, but a small contribution. It is funny what lodges in the memory from childhood.

Finally, Judson also gave me an opportunity to begin opening up to the possibility of team sports. Up to that point, I really had not done much with teams at elementary school, but now I was looking forward to giving some new things a try at my new school as I entered the seventh grade. At the time, the most I had done in terms of athletics was things like occasionally throwing a football around with friends.

Of course, there was a great reason I had not joined any competitive sports to that point; my asthma was very serious. There were times when I thought I might die because of the seriousness of some attacks. When those happened, I just wanted to hold onto something, but that didn't help me breathe. It felt like being stuck inside something and trying to pull myself out. My whole body felt as if it had too little air. I needed an inhaler, but those weren't available at the time. The doctors gave me medicine that helped. But if I woke up in the middle of the night and started having an asthma attack, I had to call for someone to help me take the medicine.

Aunt Vange had been very encouraging about my health, but she was no longer with me. I didn't get asthma attacks very often in Florida, but if I started acting a certain way, she would say, "OK, you've got to take the medicine now." Or she would say something like, "Let's just take it easy for a little while and you'll get better." With that no longer available, perhaps I felt it was time to expand what I could do on my own.

As it would turn out, seventh grade would be the only time I would attend Judson. When that school year ended, my parents brought me back to Long Island and enrolled me in Buckley Country Day school for my eighth-grade year. There were things I had liked at Judson and other things I didn't care for so much. Overall, I enjoyed my year there, but I was fine with not returning.

★ ★ ★

It was during these young years that certain realities slowly entered my consciousness. For example, I have never gone to public school. When I went to Florida, there were other kids there whose families also lived up north and would come down to visit them. In particular, I remember two friends I had who were twins. They were Jewish and their parents would come down from New York City to see them. I think at that point it was starting to dawn on me that the adult world divided people up in different ways, including class, wealth, and religion.

Florida being in the South and this being the late forties and early fifties, that also included the division by race, which was quite open. I vividly remember when I first got down there and walked into the "wrong" bathroom. I was quickly told, "Don't go in there. That's for the n****rs." It was completely bewildering, particularly to a child. But the adults in that world wanted to make sure that this difference they insisted upon was made starkly clear from childhood on.

Class and social distinctions were just the expectation throughout my childhood and adolescence. It was more assumed than talked about, but it was also clear in the group that my parents belonged to that it was expected that your children would attend an Ivy League school or something near that level. You also should belong to the right clubs, and make sure you were listed in the Social Register.

Today, the Social Register is no big deal. In the first half of the twentieth century, it meant a great deal to many people, including my family and the circles they moved within. It would be looked at and read. Now people hardly bother with it or worry who is in it. Neither of my sisters are listed and my brother is mentioned because he married somebody who was in it. The importance of those kinds of things has changed over time and lessened significantly.

Growing up, belonging to this social class did make me proud but it also gave me a sense of uncertainty. Some of the guys I knew attended the very top schools like Exeter or Andover. At some point, these kids were going to good private schools on Long Island and beginning to have dances. Because I had been away for so long, I felt a little on the outside. I usually did get a slot for most of the dances, but I really didn't have the social finesse for that kind of thing. Going to Buckley Country Day School brought me back into the Long Island social groups and made me more aware of what conferred status.

I was only at Buckley Country Day for one year, and it was a challenging time for me. I didn't get close to anybody. Some students were the sons of my parents' friends, and I would see them on other occasions, so that helped some, but I still felt like a bit of an outsider that year.

Long Island during that time was interesting. My parents belonged to several clubs in Long Island. It was a different and more unique world than you would experience today. For example, my mom liked pheasant shooting. They had trap shooting and skeet shooting at Piping Rock Country Club, so we joined that for a year or two. Dad also golfed often at Meadowbrook Club and was quite good at it.

There were ways you were socialized into your class; for instance that was the time when I started going to dancing lessons. I saw people there, although not frequently. As I got older, I'd see neighbors at football games and other events, but I didn't know them well. While I saw them socially, I often felt we were in competition.

I wasn't quite sure of myself. Once, I really wanted to get a date with one girl, but this other guy, who looked like Cary Grant, was my competition. I knew she was going to go out with him if he asked. I just didn't know how to compete with that. I felt a bit backward for some time.

After eighth grade ended at Buckley, my parents did what most families who were part of the North Shore Long Island group did—sent the kids away to boarding school to get a great education. Private school might be expensive, but the hope was it would be your ticket to an Ivy League college.

My parents applied to a couple of places. One of those was The Hotchkiss School, a well-known and renowned boarding school in Connecticut. My dad had gone there before he went to Yale, but I wasn't accepted because my grades weren't quite good enough for that highly competitive school.

I was accepted at Canterbury in New Milford, Connecticut where my dad's younger brother had gone, and it was decided that is where I would attend. My parents drove me to the school. Initially, I was moved into a double room with another guy from Buckley Day School. But I felt that I couldn't be in a double room with this guy for a full school year. It had much less to do with him than me.

I didn't dislike him, but at that time in my life, I guess I needed some solitude and quiet. Mom and Dad talked to the school, and they got me a single room for my freshman year, which was helpful for me in making the adjustment.

One of my most vivid memories from Canterbury was the Catholic rituals we attended regularly. Thinking back, I remember there was only one priest among the faculty, which is a little surprising at a Catholic school. He was our chaplain and lived on campus, but wasn't a teacher. We attended Mass once a week in addition to Sunday, and we were told if we did things wrong, we were expected to go to Confession.

I remember liking the Masses at Canterbury, which perhaps was a little unusual for my age. On Sundays, we would sing. That's where I really got into singing, and liked it enough to join the choral group at Canterbury. We were singing hymns in Latin as well as English. Our choral group would travel and sing at Catholic schools in the area.

After a childhood where my asthma often kept me from competing in sports, I wanted to find some form of athletics where I could excel. I tried out for soccer. But most of the team had played before at other schools, so my skill level was not up to the others. There was a football team, but at that time I was 5 feet, 10 inches and weighed only about 150 pounds.

The swimming team was more promising for me, so I gave it a shot. It turned out to be a good option, because if you have asthma, swimming is the best sport; it requires you to breathe in and out more often and more heavily than normal. That helps expand your lungs. At this point, my asthma was still affecting me a little, especially if there was a lot of pollen. But by then we had atomizers, so I was more comfortable pushing myself more.

So, I went out for swimming. It wasn't a particularly great swimming team, and we had an old-fashioned pool. Still, my senior year I was elected co-captain with another guy, even though neither one of us was a fantastic swimmer. We did okay in some competitions. For my own health, the most important thing was that swimming did indeed help expand my lungs.

As far as other leadership positions, I wanted to be one of four guys in my class that were Sacristans—the students who served as a kind of liaison between the chaplain and the students. I was never appointed one.

Nor was I selected as a Proctor, which entailed watching over school behavior and ensuring that guys in the boarding house weren't acting up. I complained about not being selected, and the faculty created a Proctor position for me, the Dining Hall Proctor. At least it was something I could put in the yearbook. Striving to be involved and developing leadership was important to me now, and these were the first steps.

I also managed to get in some trouble. Once at Canterbury, I plotted with two friends to ring the Chapel bell in the middle of the night, something that obviously wasn't allowed. Afterward, the head of the school made it clear that the guilty party needed to come forward or the whole school would face repercussions. One of my co-conspirators decided to take the rap, and told us, "I'll do it for both of you guys." He did, and he was punished, an admirable example of falling on one's sword for others.

When you became a senior at Canterbury, you were allowed to go to the movies, but we had to go into New Milford with a teacher as a chaperone. There were certainly different rules back then compared to anything you would see today.

Another example is the formality expected as young men and young women would meet. As part of the choral group at Canterbury, I would go on trips to the girls' schools to sing.

A particularly memorable trip happened at a Marymount school. To give you a window on how things were done then, the Mother Superior at the school wrote to our headmaster, Mr. Sheehan, and asked if he could send her a list of the boys who would be attending, what grade they were in, and how tall each one was.

So, the boys from Canterbury arrived at Marymount, and the nun who's in charge of the event says, "OK, young men, go to the stairs and line up at the top right, shortest to tallest." The girls lined up on the left stairs in the same manner; all of this was to align us by height to best pair us up.

So we start out, and the shortest guy comes out on his side, and the girl comes from the other side, and they start walking down the stairs together. The others are following them, and this continues.

I'm toward the back, because by that time, I'm close to six feet. There's a guy in front of me, and he was the type who was pretty sure of himself. When he looked at the girl across from him, he stopped on a step while all the girls kept moving down the stairs.

He checks out at the next girl, and apparently he decides he likes her looks better. So he starts walking again, choosing this girl while ignoring the first one who was intended as his match.

I started thinking, *Wait a minute, what did he just do?* But I kept going. I'm sure the poor girl he let go ahead felt like, "What's wrong with me?" Of course, there was nothing wrong with her, the guy had just acted rudely.

As a result, Mr. Sheehan talked to my impolite classmate and I'm not sure what was done to him when he got back to school. But I'm pretty sure that the nuns at Marymount never used that lineup method again.

There were some very good teachers at Canterbury. Some had been there for twenty or thirty years. My sophomore year, I took a course in medieval history. The teacher was named Roderick Clark. He had a master's degree and had gone to Canterbury and then on to college. He had an accident after college; he was paralyzed from the waist down.

He used crutches; I don't think I ever saw him in a wheel-chair. He was very articulate, and I was fascinated with the Middle Ages. When I was growing up, I had heard stories about kings and queens, their armies, and the Middle Ages. His personality and teaching method made quite an impression on me.

You could tell Mr. Clark was sincerely enthusiastic when introducing his students to the Middle Ages. He gave us homework of course, and reading all those pages wasn't always fun; he would tell us a story in addition to that. The stories were specific and had depth to them, which helped me to see history as filled with real people, acting in ways that could be understood.

He was the kind of teacher where students always felt they could stay and ask a question after the class. He was approachable, even if it was something personal you wanted to ask.

One snowy winter day, after leaving his classroom, I was walking behind him on a pathway that had frozen over. Mr. Clark was on his crutches. He was a little ahead of me when one of the crutches slipped and he fell down. I rushed up to ask if I could help. But he said, without a trace of anger or self-pity, "No, that's all right." I stood there and watched as he got his crutches, pulled himself up, and kept walking.

As I followed him, I thought to myself, *He is a great teacher.* There was something truly impressive in the dignity with which he pulled himself up. Some years after I graduated, he became Headmaster at Canterbury.

I don't think I completely realized it myself at the time, but here was a man who taught me by example of getting up and succeeding despite difficulties. Subconsciously I thought to myself, *There's a guy who really works at success, and he can do it.* That thought hit me like a ton of bricks. It made me realize, "Hey, I can do better if I work at it too."

CHAPTER 7

YALE

IT WAS AT CANTERBURY THAT THE PRESSURE OF COLLEGE admissions began to press down on me a bit. Yale was my top choice. My grandfather Pa Ewing was an alum, but I think it was my dad's stories about the place that clinched it for me. It had played a big part in his life, and I sensed his time at Yale had been among his best years.

However, I had to get admitted first, and I knew that meant building my resume. I think I was in my junior year at Canterbury, when I realized I needed to make a bid to captain a sports team, to earn a Proctor's title, and get as many distinctions on my record as possible. It seemed important to be captain of a sports team or to proctor other services.

Yale was of course taking people from schools like Andover and Exeter, the top private schools. Canterbury at that time was no doubt a quality school, but in comparison with the heavy hitters, it was considered more middle of the road.

As it turns out, three people of the forty-five in my class were accepted to Yale; I was thrilled to be one of them. My father and grandfather attending probably helped my resume quite a bit, as legacy was a factor in admissions. Whatever the reason, I was happy to be on my way.

Despite that good news, there was also a lot of sadness swirling around in the family. This was the same time when my parents were getting a divorce and my dad's drinking was not getting any better. Normally, given his history with Yale, it would have been his role to drive me up to New Haven.

Instead, that responsibility fell to my mother. I was the first to arrive in my dorm room, and I remember being a little overwhelmed—the campus seemed big to me. I was surprised to feel upset saying goodbye to my mother, but she was encouraging and told me, "You're going to have a wonderful time here."

When Dad had talked about Yale, it was his social life that stood out. I remember seeing him with friends from those days, and it seemed like it was an ideal life. He enjoyed the fraternities, the sports, and the classes. He had been the football team manager and captain of the rugby team. I wanted to dive in and build those memories and friendships too.

So, dive in I did. I remember during my freshman year William F. Buckley came to speak. Being somewhat conservative, I attended and joined a political group.

I wanted to sing, but when I tried out for the song club,

they told me that while I had a good natural voice, I needed some training. I also tried out for the swimming team. I knew I wasn't the greatest in the world, but I thought I was good enough to make the team.

The swim team coaching staff discovered an issue with my spine, and I was told I had to straighten out my back. The swim coach gave me certain exercises to do, and if they didn't work, they wouldn't take me on the team. It did not seem to be working out with swimming, so I kept searching. A friend of mine was on a rowing team, and I was able to join him with the lightweight crew team. Training expectations and time commitments were taxing, but I had discovered something I enjoyed.

The rowing team was also the gateway to a unique spiritual experience in my life. The scene was the Hudson River in New York City. At the time, I was on the junior varsity, and we were competing in a meet against Columbia University and University of Pennsylvania.

When you row, you have someone calling out the cadence, so everyone stays in sync. I recall it being a particularly beautiful day, with the sun reflecting off the water and tourists on a Circle Line boat smiling and waving at us. We were rowing exceptionally well together, and everyone was on the same page.

Arriving first over the finish line, a strange but incredibly calm feeling came over me. It felt like the universe was expanding and time stopped. And somehow I knew, felt it in my bones, that this is a wonderful world. It was almost like God was there, but not right in front of me. I have often wondered if it was the Holy Spirit manifesting in my life for the briefest of moments.

And it really was brief—it was a matter of seconds. But all these decades later, it is still a vivid memory and has been helpful in my spiritual life. The importance of an experience is not necessarily related to how long it lasted.

★ ★ ★

Rowing was not my only extracurricular activity. During my sophomore year, I joined the same fraternity my dad had belonged to. I also brought in a cousin of mine who was from St. Louis. Being in a fraternity was a mixed bag from my perspective. It became clear that there was an inner group within the fraternity of the extremely elite and wealthy. We were all "brothers," but some brothers were more equal than others. On the flip side, the fraternity had good parties and that was a lot of fun.

Something else important happened to me while I was a senior at Yale. I went to visit my sister, Tara, who was attending Sarah Lawrence College and it was there I first met the woman who would become my wife, Margot. However, it was not love at first sight.

Fate would give us a second chance during the winter of 1965. By happenstance, both of our families traveled for a ski trip to the same town in Switzerland. It was a beautiful setting and things blossomed. The following winter our families returned to the same spot, and that cemented our relationship. Some months later, I attended Margot's and Tara's graduation at Sarah Lawrence, and then on June 23, 1967, our families and friends joined us for our wedding at Holy Angels Parish in Dayton, Ohio. Saying yes is the best decision I have ever made.

Now it was time to choose a career and get to work.

CHAPTER 8

A CAREER IN BANKING

IN MY SENIOR YEAR AT YALE, I PLANNED TO ATTEND graduate school and become a history professor. My Graduate School Boards were okay but they weren't quite good enough to get me into Harvard, Stanford, or Yale in this field.

Looking back, I realize that I could easily have attended one of the many other perfectly good graduate schools but I thought the best professors came out of Stanford and the Ivies. I decided that if I couldn't go to one of them, there were other career paths available.

I was fortunate to have options and considered other possibilities. I even flirted with the idea of joining the Peace Corps but after some reflection decided that wasn't the right fit.

Two of my Yale roommates had gone on to business school. In the 1960s, MBAs were becoming very popular and prestigious. Now MBAs are everywhere, but back then it was more unusual. Once again, I made it my goal to attend an Ivy League school. I didn't get into Harvard or Yale, but I was accepted from the waiting list at Columbia. After a few tutoring sessions, I took the Business Boards again and this time I got in.

Having entered Columbia in the fall of 1965, I look back and question if it was the right decision. I would come out as one of those young people with a great education, but no real world experience. Now it seems more common to take a few years off between college and business school.

If I had taken some time off from school, I could have learned more about working environments and how the business world actually operates, and then gone back to school with that experience as context.

Instead, by going straight into graduate school, I learned all the most modern theories and practices but had little hands-on experience. I came out thinking I knew better than most of my bosses, which I quickly learned wasn't true at all.

The business curriculum at Columbia was a two-year program. During the time I was there, I worked during the summer months. I took an internship with Citibank and through the kindness of my Uncle Lewis B. Harder, I became a security guard at the largest underground gold mine in Columbia.

Coming out of school, I then applied to and interviewed with several banks and was offered a few positions. Earlier that year, I had contacted my Pa Ewing for advice. It was fortunate I was able to speak to him when I did before he passed away the following spring. He advised me that if I wanted to work internationally, Citibank was my best option. My application with Citibank was accepted and I joined the organization with a lot of other young people. I was the only one who held an MBA.

This was a rewarding time for me. Everything was coming together nicely, and I felt like the future was all laid out for me. I had gotten married and found a job. After our wedding, Margot and I took a long honeymoon to Ireland, the UK, and Paris. It was after we got home that I found out Citibank had hired me.

Upon our return, we had to wait to find out where I would be assigned. I started to grow a bit nervous as other newly hired people were getting assigned overseas and time was marching on. In the interval, we lived in a rent-controlled apartment in New York not far from the United Nations building. Dad was still working in real estate at the time and had found the apartment for us. It was close to my job at Citibank and Margot was able to take a bus to her job at the Rockefeller Institute.

We were quite excited when I finally received my assignment to San Salvador, the capital of El Salvador. The initial plan had been to send me to Guatemala, but there was some delay in opening a branch there.

When I arrived in San Salvador in the fall of 1968, I was a very junior bank officer. There was still some necessary training I needed. I was put in charge of the bank tellers and their cash drawers. The tellers of course were required to balance out every night before we left. One evening, the numbers weren't balancing, and we couldn't find the error. By about 6:15 p.m., the tellers were asking me if it would be okay to leave things unbalanced and return early the next morning to find the error.

I stood firm and told them, "I'm sorry guys, but you know we have to work this out. There may be other problems in the morning that we'll have to focus on. I don't want to have to explain this to the manager."

Eventually, after another half an hour of searching, we found the mistake and were able to balance the books and go home. When I returned early the next morning, before the bank had even opened, I noticed two men in dark suits waiting at the door. They were auditors from New York. Thankfully, we had balanced the books the night before and everything was in good order. Had that discrepancy still been there, it might have done significant damage to my working comrades and my fledgling career.

As I mentioned earlier, this was an eventful time in my life, none more so than the month of July 1969, when war broke out, my son was born, my father died, and the first moon landing happened.

Another thing I clearly remember from my time in Central America were the extremes of economic status. My grandmother, Dorothy, had a friend she had known for many years who was a member of what was known as the "Catorce"—the richest fourteen families in El Salvador who made up that country's elite.

Grandmother wrote her friend a letter introducing Margot and me. Mrs. G. invited us to dinner one evening. There were fourteen of us at the table and every single person had a servant standing in attendance behind their chair.

It was such a contrast from what I witnessed elsewhere in the country. Mrs. G. lived in a nice part of San Salvador but there were also parts of the city where the streets weren't safe at all. Even now, more than fifty years later, the entire country is more insecure. It seems my oldest son, Jamie, will never be able to visit the country where he was born. One of the nephews of Mrs. G. was kidnapped and held for ransom. He never made it home—he was tortured and killed by his kidnappers.

After living in El Salvador, I still to this day think to myself how fortunate I have been. To see the poverty and crime all around the world is sobering. Working as a bank official, I wasn't exposed to the desperately poor very often because banking centers were typically in well-off parts of cities. Occasionally we would travel to other towns, and the poverty was disheartening.

I also began to realize how fortunate I was to have parents and grandparents who preceded me and who were able to give me an extra step up in life. I know most people never get that. It was only a small portion of us who had been given that kind of head start, and I was grateful to those who came before me.

We left El Salvador for good at the end of 1969. We returned to New York and then I went to Puerto Rico for eighteen months. Fidel Castro had just come to power in Cuba, so a number of wealthy and successful Cubans were seeking asylum in Puerto Rico. Some Puerto Ricans were biased against them, but I worked with several Cubans at our bank, and I found them to be smart and hard working.

It was in Puerto Rico when I began to realize that sometimes working in a bank can force you to make some hard ethical decisions. At one point, the staff was asked by bank officers to contribute to one of Puerto Rico's two or three political parties. We were assured by the officers that we would be reimbursed for our contributions. I knew there was something wrong with this, so I went to my boss and stated that I didn't think this was right, mentioning that some of us might feel differently about the particular candidate that the bank officers wanted to support.

I also added that I felt very uncomfortable about getting paid back for a political contribution. The officer I spoke with told me there were reasons it was done that way but suggested I speak with the regional vice president. I did that and as I was speaking with him, I realized that this was going to be considered standard policy. Everybody else on staff was doing it and I thought that if I protested anymore, I could very well lose my job. So, I made the decision to live with my uneasiness and contributed.

After I returned from Puerto Rico, I decided to join the private banking sector of Citibank. I'm very happy I did that. With private banking, you are able to deal with the customers personally. You work with them, their investments, and their assets. There's also a bit of travel involved. Working in private banking also reminded me of how my grandfather had set up irrevocable trusts for his future generations. I found it rewarding that I could do something similar for people overseas who might otherwise not have known about assets and estate planning.

I met my first customer in Mexico City. He was a nice gentleman who invited me over for dinner on a Friday with his Jewish family. Several weeks later, he stopped by in New York and made a fixed time deposit in the bank, an early success for me.

★ ★ ★

The next step on my path happened in 1976. Citibank was opening a private bank in Southeast Asia and they asked me if I would be interested in going there. I asked Margot and, despite it being a big move for the whole family, she supported me. We went to Singapore for five years. It would turn out to be the best assignment of my career.

Living in Singapore gave unique opportunities for business encounters. My first exploration from my new Southeast Asia base was to Brunei. I met with an Englishman, an advisor to the Sultan of Brunei. It was almost impossible to meet with the Sultan himself. The Sultan, about my age, was quite wealthy and had recently purchased about ninety polo ponies from Argentina. Unfortunately, his family wasn't interested in dealing with Americans. They only did business with the English banks. A few years later, a bright Citibank colleague was able to figure out a way to get a working relationship going by donating outstanding trophies for the winning team of the annual Brunei Polo Match.

Singapore also gave all of us distinctive opportunities for friendship, and an interesting education for our children. Margot's charming group of English, Dutch, French, and Italian ladies not only made some fascinating cultural and shopping trips to Burma and India, but arranged some entertaining local parties as well.

Our three children, Jamie, Michael, and Shelley, were seven, five, and three when we arrived in Asia. We needed to find a suitable school for them. With the Singapore American School reeling from two senior students being caught with a small supply of marajuana, we were advised to enroll our children in Tanglin Trust Schools, created on the British educational model. Tanglin turned out to be an excellent choice, and we grew to appreciate the positives within the English system of education.

The kids had some options for leisure, with a soccer league for six- and seven-year-olds, as well as Little League Baseball backed by the American and Canadian families associated with offshore oil rigs.

With Margot and the kids doing well, I was happy to be

traveling to Indonesia, Malaysia, and Thailand visiting "high-net-worth individuals" to help them set up accounts to protect and manage their personal assets. Local Citibank branches assisted in introductions to business owners in Jakarta, Kuala Lumpur, and Bangkok. Invariably the potential and actual clients were Chinese families, part of a minority population whose business success was watched closely by the governments of those countries.

Time and personal values took on a greater meaning as I grew into my role. I also had the advice of local friends plus more experienced bank associates, which helped me build more patience and perspective. I found myself learning a lot through both mistakes and differing viewpoints.

You had to learn to find your way through different cultural ideals. Dining with two lovely dining partners instead of choosing one, along with politely rejecting gifts that went against your own standards, were two dance steps I had to navigate along my journey.

While it is always a little rough launching an office in a new place, fortunately my boss and the head office held their breath and gave us time. It paid off when our account growth picked up in 1979. By the spring of 1981, I was reassigned to the bank in New York, leaving the office responsibility to Romano Babini, a charming and effective Swiss Italian who substantially increased the client relationships.

After several conversations with my seniors in New York, I was appointed as head of international marketing for

US commercial properties, such as office buildings and shopping centers. After reviewing the viability of a property sale, our group would create and distribute a well-edited investment brochure. Working with staff contacting European, Asian, and Latin American clients, we would put together the purchase and administration of the property for the client/owner.

Unfortunately by 1988, international investors looked directly to local real estate brokers, eliminating for them the additional time and costs of a bank's fiduciary investment procedure. Working as a marketing intermediate between the sellers and the investors was becoming less and less viable. I was laid off.

Things were difficult after I left the bank. It was not pleasant having your career trajectory changed and suddenly facing having to find something else. Initially, I thought it would be fairly easy to find a similar job at another bank. My record was good, and I certainly had a history of dealing with excellent clients. But most of the banks I interviewed with wanted me to bring those clients with me, and I felt very uneasy about doing business that way. It was a somewhat common practice, but taking clients in that manner did not feel right to me.

Slowly, I came to realize that I should look elsewhere for employment. I was on the board of the Mercantile Library of New York and had done quite a bit of nonprofit work with them. I enjoyed that. As a board member, I learned how nonprofits operated. At one point, I became involved with the library and was able to look after the finances—which weren't doing well. We realized there were probably too many librarians working, so we let one of the assistants go. Then the head librarian left, and there was this vacancy to fill. Because I'd had banking experience, the board asked me if I would take over temporarily as the head of the library, and I agreed. It felt good to help clean up the finances and help the library go in the right direction.

We eventually found someone who was very good at organization, and I was able to move on from that temporary role. I soon found another job with a nonprofit called Council for Aid to Education. The organization was small, about ten people, and it focused on education research. I was with them for some time but as it turned out, the donations weren't coming in as planned. They were looking at cutting staff, so I moved on to another nonprofit type of job that was involved with research and development.

During this time, I became quite active in several civic-type organizations such as the Retired Men's Association. Getting involved with our children's school in Greenwich, I became a Trustee of Brunswick School, working with the school activities committee. It was and is a fine private high school for boys with an excellent faculty and top quality athletic facilities.

Even with the satisfaction and enjoyment of working in the nonprofit sector, one of its key components did not suit me particularly well. Nonprofit work involved a constant need to raise money, and that just was not a fit for my personality.

So, I began to think about going back for education, possibly to do more work related to banking. Thanks to the trusts arranged by William Ewing for the families' third generation, Margot, Shelley, Jamie, Michael, and I had the financial breathing room to take the time to find the next step forward.

This was my state of career flux in the fall of 1994. Then the boating accident happened, and everything was suddenly different. I found myself no longer worrying about my career, and instead fought for my life.

CHAPTER 9

RECOVERY AND RESILIENCE

I WISH I COULD SAY THAT AFTER I SURVIVED THAT TER-rible boating accident in the fall of 1994 and woke up in the hospital, that it was a speedy recovery back to the time before the accident. But of course, it was a long journey and not always a straight path.

To give you some idea of where I was starting from when I first regained consciousness, Margot says she was told my brain had taken such a heavy blow that I had been knocked back to a second-grade mentality. At the time, I had a very limited ability to read and write.

Once I was discharged, I had to go through a six-month rehabilitation period that included everything from phys-ical therapy to education. My brain had to be retrained to bring me back to a more adult state of mind. I was for-tunate to have a specialist who worked with me for some time. I do not remember everything he did—it was more than a quarter of a century ago by now—but I do remember we worked on all kinds of tests. Of course, this kind of care was expensive. Mom paid for all of it, something I still look back upon with tremendous gratitude.

As I started to get better and come out of it, a couple of things happened. I learned that I am what is known as a single-tasking personality, and that would be a permanent effect of the injury I sustained. That means I am able to concentrate and dedicate myself to one thing at a time. As an example, if I'm working on a particular project at my desk, then somebody comes in to see me about an urgent matter, and on top of that, the phone rings with another bid for my attention, I would struggle mightily with all that coming at me at once. Single-tasking is not anything I would ask for of course, but it is manageable. Combining alarms, reminders, and computers while developing habits helps set up a process to respond to the current and future actions.

I also discovered that I had to go through a process of relearning how to learn. And not only how to learn, but then how to retain what I learned in my memory. It was a long and frustrating process at times. My recall ability was significantly decreased for some time.

One mark of progress was the day I was able to retake the Connecticut driver's license exam and have my license restored. After the accident, the license had been canceled because of my mental age. It may sound like a rather ordinary thing, but I can assure you when a document like a driver's license is taken from you, you feel a serious loss has occurred. The day I got the license back was a very happy day.

When circumstances put you in a deep hole, you appreciate every bit of progress on your way back to the surface. Being grateful and celebrating progress is a path to help recover from suffering that may occur. It is not an easy path but it is one that helps remove negative aspects.

It also took about six months to improve to the extent that I was able to start talking to lawyers. Margot and my Uncle Bill had already spoken with a couple of lawyers, but we were looking for someone in Greenwich or Stamford. The family office was in New York. Research and references were reviewed resulting in choosing Silver, Golub, and Teitel. It was a fortunate choice. It was a tough, long case, but through the efforts of Mr. Silver and his colleagues, we were able to win a judgment against the guilty parties.

The case ended up taking seven years in the courts. Given the nature of our legal system and this kind of case, that may not seem like an unreasonable amount of time. But I can tell you from my perspective, it felt like a painfully long time for the case to remain unresolved. While that case was ongoing, both our lawyers and my psychologist recommended that I gradually begin to move back into society.

My advisers suggested that I gradually ease my way back into that sort of position that I had in my career before the accident, something in banking or the nonprofit sector. But I certainly was not ready to start there.

My first job post-accident was with a company called Kinko's. Bought out by FedEx in 2004, the company specialized in office services. I worked as a counter person, doing simple tasks. I enjoyed the work, in large part because Kinko's was a place where my coworkers had all kinds of different backgrounds. We worked together as a team and served customers from all walks of life.

It was also helpful having this job when my case came to court, because the lawyers would be able to show that I was trying to get back into the world again. But it was also strange going from my previous career with a high-paying bank job to working for eight dollars an hour.

It was a difficult and frightening time, but my lawyer reassured us that he'd seen a lot of people recover from head injuries. He was more comforting than the doctors, who refused to ever predict anything. Mr. Silver gave both me and Margot faith that I would come around and be myself again.

And he was right. Gradually, after those six months of rehabilitation, we began to see the light. A spark was back, and it felt amazing! The doctors were so relieved that throughout these many months, I had never developed a blood clot. That would have killed me instantly. The medication I was given did its job and both healed the injury and dried the blood.

Despite many of the doctors being hesitant to make predictions, one of my doctors was always so kind to us and helped us understand the long-term consequences. Margot once said, "When the doctor helped our family recognize that this was going to be the way Jim was, we all sort of rallied. It gave the family a lot more togetherness and strength that we never knew we had in us."

This is a demonstration again of the idea that when you need to draw on reservoirs of resilience, the key ingredients come from family. Our children were also affected by the accident—maybe in some ways even more than we were. To this day, my daughter is very concerned about accidents. She worries about her own two boys. Our son, Michael, avoids talking about it. The accident was so life changing, that we often measure time by saying things like, "Oh, that was before the accident," or "That happened after the accident."

Of course, it's not just family you rely on. Sometimes you find just the right kind of person who fills a big need. During my convalescence, we had a wonderful Chilean woman, Margarita, who came every day to take care of me. She was my mainstay since Margot, unfortunately, had to keep working to ensure we kept our medical insurance.

Margarita would come at eight o'clock in the morning and she stayed until Margot returned at 2:00 p.m. Margarita didn't talk a lot, but she gave me lunch and took me on walks. We had another individual who would drive me up to my rehab appointments in Norwalk. It was all because of the generous caregiving of so many that we made it through every day.

So many people supported us during that time, and it

helped strengthen my religious faith. There were Catholic priests, including Father Gilbert, Monsignor Alan, and Father Bill who were especially helpful.

At that time, going to church itself was a breath of fresh air. It reinforced for me that the Catholic Church can be a kind of second home, a comforting thought that has occurred to me many times in my life. Being unable to drive, I relied on Margot and some of our friends to get me there.

Margot has often remarked that one of the reasons I pulled through all of this was because of my belief in God and the Catholic Church. I have always had a strong faith, even before the accident. It's been a constant part of life.

My wife has also noted that I was so grateful to be alive when I woke up in the hospital; it's likely that I believed the Church was my new calling. That would explain my habit of blessing everyone I saw while I was a patient there during my stay!

There is an interesting bookend to this story of an accident that deepened my ideas of resilience, family, and faith. I ended up in a role that was very similar to the role I had dreamed up for myself after the accident.

At one point after my recovery was well underway, I was introduced to a fellow Catholic and Knight of Malta named Victor Coudert who also lived in Greenwich. After learning of my volunteer work, he suggested that I may be interested in becoming a Eucharistic Minister at the hospital. Eucharistic Ministers visit patients, can administer communion, and may assist a priest with administering other sacraments.

I decided to take the suggestion and went through the necessary training. At the hospital, I was under the guidance of the Catholic Chaplin. I would visit patients on several floors and ask how they were feeling and if they would like to pray and receive the Eucharist. Some said yes, some said no, but it all felt pastoral, and I got a sense of peace from it.

A few times when I would go into a room and offer the Host to a patient, they would tell me they wanted to take communion but hadn't been to church or confession in years. One man wanted to give me his confession—which as a layperson, I of course could not do. It seems I was still being mistaken for a priest in the hospital!

It was an extremely fulfilling role for me, and it reinforced for me the importance of caring for others. No matter what sufferings are visited upon you, when you can focus on giving to someone else, it helps ease your own burdens because you forget about them.

The accident was, of course, a terrible thing. When I woke up in that hospital, in that little room, I didn't know where I was or what I had lost. But now it is a part of my life, and it taught me deep lessons about resilience, and it made me return to the fundamentals of my life. It also helped me pause to consider my own life and the generations that came before me, and how grateful I am for my family and its history.

EPILOGUE

I AVOID TELLING OTHERS WHAT TO THINK OR HOW TO live because I don't believe I have all the answers. While I would like to think eight decades of living have given me at least some wisdom, preaching at others is not something I am comfortable with. That's why this book has not been written as self help or with overconfident pronouncements about how you should live.

Even so, I do have the modest hope that this book will have some value for readers beyond mere interest in the story of a family and a life. I thought it might be worthwhile to add an epilogue to reflect on three of the themes in the book that might provide some help for readers on their own journeys through life.

When I look at my life and those who have come before and after me, you cannot help but see some tough times. They happen to us all, even those fortunate enough to be born into money and the education and privilege that comes with it.

During those harder times—and sometimes even in the good times—it can be challenging to get perspective on life. My hope is that the long view of this book, looking at life through the lens of generations, can help you find that perspective. If you can recognize yourself and your own family in it, maybe that will help you feel a little more connected and at peace with your life.

Upon reflection of all the pages that came before, I see three key insights that may help others as they navigate through life. One insight is that cultivating faith yields comfort and strength when you need it most. A common faith can serve as a thread that ties together families through generations.

Another insight is that we need to be mindful of the impact we have on others. Our actions do not just influence the here and now, but also reverberate through the generations. We should be aware of that impact and strive to make it a positive one.

The final insight is that we all have the power to be resilient, and that we can come out of experiences of great suffering and still find joyful times and live for a purpose.

Here is a final reflection on each of these insights.

CULTIVATING FAITH

In looking back on both sides of my family, the Roman Catholic Church has been a constant. One of my great-grandfather James Butler's stated life goals was to "add to the glory of the Catholic Church." He did this through his charitable giving and other actions. With his cousin, Mother Marie Joseph Butler, he also helped found the Marymount schools.

My grandfather William Ewing (or "Pa" as his grandkids called him) was similarly inclined to support the Roman Catholic Church with his philanthropy.

Of course, faith has also been a bulwark in my own life. Family conflicts, my accident, and the injuries sustained tested my own beliefs. In many ways, these moments brought it out more clearly. Difficult times tend to do that.

Life is always going to have its share of disappointments, struggles, and loss. Both my father and his father suffered from problems with alcohol; both also met early deaths. My own accident forced me to consider once more the impact of the good, the bad, and the ugly occurrences in life. I have watched family members and friends live their own lives and move forward.

Through everything life brings, faith can be a stable ground to help you continue growing. I'm not one to preach on street corners or push any kind of religious beliefs on others, recognizing that there are always stones in the pathway of any spiritual belief.

But I still think that faith is an indispensable aid for living a good and meaningful life. Perhaps after reading this, you'll consider the importance of strengthening an existing faith or returning to a faith. Whatever that might mean in your own life, it is something to ponder and then take action on. You may find that moments of relief will appear.

BE MINDFUL OF YOUR IMPACT ON OTHERS

Every choice we make toward others can have lasting impact. Living day to day, we can easily forget that our actions should match our values.

I think of the clashes in my own father's life about how wealth would be handed down in the Butler family, and the negative impact that had on him. I contrast that with the good fruit that grew from the trusts set up by my Grandfather Ewing. His was a more equal way to pass down wealth. William Ewing had the foresight and care to think generationally and to realize it was in his power to look out for those who would come after him.

Of course, our impact on others goes much deeper than money. I think, for example, of Aunt Vange, my caretaker in Florida during my childhood years battling asthma. Aunt Vange could have simply been a somewhat indifferent caretaker, someone just "doing her job" of taking care of a child.

But she treated it as much more than that. She went beyond a simple caretaker and looked out for my emotional, developmental, and spiritual needs. I was only with her for a relatively short time in my life, but her impact on me has been lifelong.

I think also of my history teacher who lost the full use of

his legs at a young age from a car accident. He would have had every right to pity himself and to let that accident derail his life; instead, he became an example of dignity and achievement for countless young people, first as a teacher and later as a headmaster.

When I think back on these experiences and others, it reminds me that what we do and how we treat others does matter. Every action we take, big and small, can impact others in ways we don't always understand at the moment. Striving to be the person who thoughtfully looks out for others and respects their dignity can give our lives purpose and meaning.

RESILIENCE

I was born into a family that gave me a significant head start in life. Of course, that included both money and education. Growing up, Dad and Mom were able to afford fine houses, excellent medical care, and nice vacations. I was educated privately and proceeded on to two Ivy League schools. I then went onto a career in international banking. I am grateful for all that good fortune and always keep it in mind.

But all that did not protect me from bouts of severe asthma as a child, an illness that had me living away from my family for long stretches to breathe easier in places like Arizona and Florida.

It did not protect me from seeing the toll my dad's abuse of alcohol had on the family, and it didn't keep me from witnessing many struggles and sufferings among family and friends.

The advantages I was born with certainly didn't protect me from the near deadly accident that temporarily knocked my cognition back to that of a child. Thankfully I recovered most of my faculties; it still made a lasting impact.

This book is not just a list of the good, the bad, and the ugly within several generations of two upper-middle-class families. I think one of the most important things to learn about in our life is that we all have the ability to develop resilience. When we are going through hard times, we sometimes feel it will never end, or that we will not be able to find our way back to more stable and happier times. Surviving tough times requires patience and determination, two of the key ingredients of resilience. We also cannot do it without others. Family, friends, and faith all matter in helping us along our road.

Without my wife Margot to help me after the accident, I do not know what I would have done. My mother had her weaknesses, and we did not always see eye to eye, but when the accident happened, she came through, visited, and helped with medical expenses. Her brother, my Uncle Bill, also was there for me.

It is in family history that we find the inner reserves that we did not know we had. Over time, we may discover that we have more resilience than we realized we were capable of. We can get through more than we thought and come out the other side, older and hopefully, a touch wiser.

ACKNOWLEDGMENTS

I WOULD LIKE TO ACKNOWLEDGE THE WONDERFUL SUP-
port and advice that has helped me bring together visions
of the past and present, translated into words and images. I
hope this family story will help others reflect on their own
lives, particularly the younger generations.

My parents, James and Jessie Butler, brought me into a
world that was struggling to preserve peace and democ-
racy while in the throes of World War II. Their dedication
to my health and education was always present despite
some hard times.

Recovery from a life-altering accident is a long journey.
Writing a book is also a long journey. I could not have
completed either journey without the support of my wife
Margot. For her amazing energy, good sense of humor, and
Midwestern steadiness, I am deeply grateful.

I would also like to acknowledge and thank the authors

of the following publications, which helped me fill in my family's story and support my own memories:

Real Lace: America's Irish Rich by Stephen Birmingham, Harper & Row, 1973.

"The Butter and Egg Man of East View" article by Richard Miller in the *River City Journal.*

The House of Morgan: An American Banking Dynasty and the Rise of Modern Finance by Ron Chernow.

Finally I would like to thank the outstanding Scribe team of Miles, David, Natalie, Esty, and Joy. Their thoughtful, patient, and effective assistance made this book possible.

ABOUT THE AUTHOR

After graduating from Yale University and Columbia School of Business, James Butler Jr. married Margaret Herbruck and joined First National City Bank (now Citicorp) in 1967. Assignments to commercial banking took him and his family to El Salvador and Puerto Rico. After returning to the head office, he transferred to the International Investment Services Division. In 1976, he moved the family to Singapore and opened an office for Southeast Asian private clients. Returning to New York in 1981, Jim worked with several nonprofit organizations. He is now retired and living with his family in Greenwich, Connecticut.